Aunt Phil's Trunk Volume Two

Teacher Guide

Bringing Alaska's history alive!

By
Laurel Downing Bill

Special credit and much appreciation to Nicole Cruz for her diligent efforts to create the best student workbook and teacher guide available for Alaska history studies.

Aunt Phil's Trunk LLC, Anchorage, Alaska
www.auntphilstrunk.com

International Standard Book Number 978-1-940479-28-6
Printed and bound in the United States of America.

First Printing 2017
First Printing Second Edition 2017
First Printing Third Edition 2018

Photo credits on the front cover, from top left: Native shaman with totem, Alaska State Library, Case and Draper Collection, ASL-P-39-782; Eskimo boy, Alaska State Library, Skinner Foundation, ASL-P44-11-002; Prospector, Alaska State Library, Skinner Foundation, ASL-P44-03-15; Athabascan woman, Anchorage Museum of History and Art, Crary–Henderson Collection, AMHA-b62-1-571; Gold miners, Alaska State Library, Harry T.Becker Collection, ASL-P67-052; Chilkoot Pass, Alaska State Library, Eric A. Hegg Collection, ASL-P124-04; Seal hunter, Alaska State Library, George A. Parks Collection, ASL-P240-210; Women mending boat, Alaska State Library, Rev. Samuel Spriggs Collection, ASL-P320-60; Teacher photo, Alaska State Library, J. Simpson MacKinnon Photo Collection, ASL-P14-073.

TABLE OF CONTENTS

TABLE OF CONTENTS

Welcome to *Aunt Phil's Trunk Volume Two* Workbook for Students!

Read the chapters associated with each Unit. Then complete the lessons for that Unit to get a better understanding of Alaska's people and the events that helped shape Alaska's future.

I hope you enjoy your journey into Alaska's past from the years 1900 to 1912.

Laurel Downing Bill, author

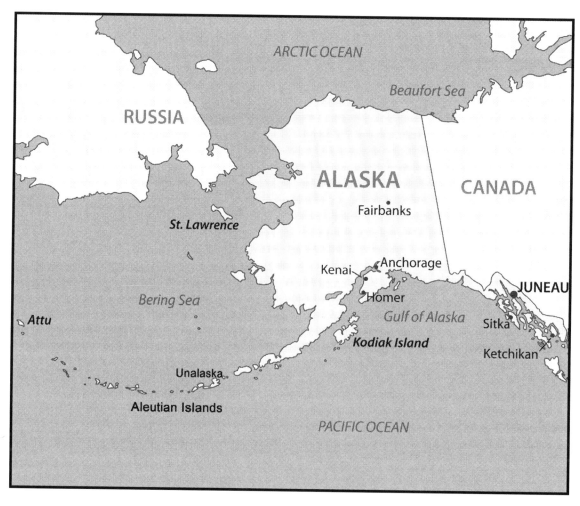

Instructions for using the *Aunt Phil's Trunk* Alaska History Curriculum

The *Aunt Phil's Trunk* Alaska History Curriculum is designed to be used in grades 4-8. High school students can use this curriculum, also, by taking advantage of the essay and enrichment activities throughout the book. The next few pages give further instruction on how to use this curriculum with middle school students, high school students and in classroom settings.

This curriculum can be taught in multiple grade levels by having your older students complete all reading, study guide work and enrichment activities independently. Students of all grade levels can participate in daily oral review by playing games like Jeopardy or Around the World.

This curriculum was developed so that students not only learn about Alaska's past, but they will have fun in the process. After every few lessons, they can test their knowledge through word scramble, word search and crossword puzzles.

Notes for parents with younger students:

Enrichment Activities occasionally direct your child to watch educational videos on YouTube.com or link to other Websites to learn more about the topic that they are reading about in the lesson. You may want to supervise younger children while they are using the Internet to be sure that they do not click on any inappropriate content. This also provides a good opportunity to discuss Internet safety with your child/children.

How to use this workbook at home

Aunt Phil's Trunk Alaska History Curriculum is designed to be used in grades 4-8. High school students can use this curriculum, also, by taking advantage of the essay and enrichment activities throughout the book. The next page gives further instruction on how to use this curriculum with high school students.

This curriculum can be taught in multiple grade levels by having your older students complete all reading, study guide work and enrichment activities independently. Students of all grade levels can participate in daily oral review by playing games like Jeopardy or Around the World.

For Middle School Students:

1. **Facts to Know:** Read this section in the study guide with your student(s) before reading the chapter to get familiar with new terms that they will encounter in the reading.

2. **Read the chapter:** Read one chapter aloud to your student(s) or have them read it aloud to you. Older students may want to read independently.

3. **Comprehension Questions:** Younger students may answer the comprehension questions orally or write down their answers in the study guide. Use these questions to test your student(s) comprehension of the chapter. Older students should answer all questions in written form.

4. **Discussion Questions:** Have your student(s) answer these questions in a few sentences orally. Come up with follow-up questions to test your student(s) understanding of the material. Older students may answer discussion questions in written essay form.

5. **Map Work:** Some chapters will contain a map activity for your student(s) to learn more about the geography of the region that they are learning about.

6. **Enrichment and Online References:** (Optional) Assign enrichment activities as you see fit. Many of the online references are from the Alaska Humanities Forum website (http://www.akhistorycourse.org). We highly recommend this website for additional information, project ideas, etc.

7. **Unit Review:** At the end of a unit, your student will complete Unit Review questions and word puzzles in the study guide. Students should review all the chapters in the unit before completing the review. Parents may want to assist younger students with the word puzzles.

8. **Unit Test:** (Optional) There is an optional test that you can administer to your student(s) after they have completed all the unit work.

How to use this workbook for high school

1. **Facts to Know:** Your student(s) should read this section in the study guide before reading the chapter to get familiar with new terms that they will encounter.

2. **Read the chapter:** Your student(s) can read aloud or independently.

3. **Comprehension Questions:** Use these questions to test your student(s) comprehension of the chapter. Have your high schoolers write out their answers in complete sentences.

4. **Discussion Questions:** Have your student(s) answer these questions in a few sentences orally or write out their answer in essay form.

5. **Map Work:** Some chapters will contain a map activity for your student(s) to learn more about the geography of the region that they are learning about.

6. **Enrichment and Online References:** Once your high schooler has completed all the reading and study guide material for the chapter, assign additional reading from the enrichment material using the online links or book lists. Encourage your student(s) to explore topics of interest to them.

Many of the online references are from the Alaska Humanities Forum website. We highly recommend this website for additional information, project ideas, etc.

7. **Unit Review:** At the end of a unit, your student will complete Unit Review questions and word puzzles in their study guide. Students should review all the chapters in the unit before completing the review.

8. **Unit Test:** (Optional) There is an optional test that you can administer to your student(s) after they have completed all the unit work.

9. **Oral Presentation:** (Optional) Assign a 5-minute oral presentation on any topic in the reading. Encourage your student(s) to utilize the additional books and online resources to supplement the information in the textbook. Set aside a classroom day for your student(s) to share their presentations.

10. **Historical Inquiry Project:** Your student(s) will choose a topic from the reading to learn more about and explore that topic through library visits, museum trips, visiting historical sites, etc.

Visit https://www.nhd.org/how-enter-contest for detailed information on how to put together a historical inquiry project. You may even want to have your students enter the national contest.

How to use this workbook in the classroom

Aunt Phil's Trunk Alaska History Curriculum was created for homeschooling families, but it also can work well in a co-op or classroom setting. Here are some suggestions on how to use this curriculum in a classroom setting. Use what works best for your classroom.

1. **Facts to Know:** The teacher introduces students to the Facts to Know to familiarize the students with terms that they will encounter in the chapter.

2. **Read the chapter:** The teacher can read the chapter aloud while the students follow along in the book. Students also may take turns reading aloud.

3. **Comprehension Questions:** The teacher uses these questions to test the students' comprehension of the chapter. Students should write out the answers in their study guide and the teacher can review the answers with the students in class.

4. **Discussion Questions:** The teacher chooses a few students to answer these questions orally during class. Alternatively, teachers can assign these questions to be completed in essay form individually and answers can be shared during class.

5. **Map Work:** Some chapters will contain a map activity for your students to learn more about the geography of the region that they are learning about. Have your students complete the activity independently.

6. **Enrichment and Online References:** Assign enrichment activities as you see fit.

7. **Daily Review:** Students should review the material for the current unit daily. You can do this by asking review questions orally. Playing review games like Jeopardy or Around the World is a fun way to get your students excited about the material.

8. **Unit Review:** At the end of a unit, your student will complete Unit Review questions and word puzzles in the study guide. Have students review all the unit chapters before completing.

9. **Unit Test:** (Optional) There is an optional test that you can administer to your students after they have completed all the unit work.

10. **Oral Presentation:** (Optional) Assign a 5-minute oral presentation on any topic in the reading. Encourage your students to utilize the additional books and online resources to supplement the information in the textbook. Set aside a classroom day for students to share their presentations.

11. **Historical Inquiry Project:** Your student(s) will choose a topic from the reading to learn more about and explore that topic through library visits, museum trips, visiting historical sites, etc.

Visit https://www.nhd.org/how-enter-contest for detailed information on how to put together a historical inquiry project. You may even want to have your students enter the national contest.

How to grade the assignments

Our rubric grids are designed to make it easy for you to grade your students' essays, oral presentations and enrichment activities. Encourage your students to look at the rubric grid before completing an assignment as a reminder of what an exemplary assignment should include.

You can mark grades for review questions, essay tests and extra credit assignments on the last page of each unit in the student workbook. Use these pages as a tool to help your students track their progress and improve their assignment grades.

Unit Review Questions

Students are given one point for each correct review and fill-in-the-blank question. Mark these points on the last page of each unit in the student workbook.

Essay Test Questions

Students will complete two or more essay questions at the end of each unit. These questions are designed to test your students' knowledge about the key topics of each unit. You can give a student up to 20 points for each essay.

Students are graded on a scale of 1-5 in four categories:

1) Understanding the topic
2) Answering all questions completely and accurately
3) Neatness and organization
4) Grammar, spelling and punctuation

Use the essay rubric grid on page 11 as a guide to give up to 5 points in each category for every essay. Mark these points for each essay on the last page of each Unit Review in the student workbook.

Word Puzzles

Word puzzles that appear at the end of the Unit Reviews count for 3 points, or you can give partial points if the student does not fill in the puzzle completely. Mark these points under the extra category on the last page of each Unit Review in the student workbook.

Enrichment Activities

Most lessons contain an enrichment activity for further research and interaction with the information in the lesson. You can make these optional or assign every activity as part of the lesson. You can use the provided rubric on page 12 to give up to 5 points for each assignment. Mark these points under the extra category on the last page of each Unit Review in the student workbook.

Oral Presentations

You have the option of assigning oral presentations on any topic from the unit as extra credit. If you choose to assign oral presentations, you can use the provided rubric to grade your student on content and presentation skills. Discuss what presentation skills you will be grading your student on before each presentation day.

Some examples of presentation skills you can grade on include:

– Eye contact with the audience
– Proper speaking volume
– Using correct posture
– Speaking clearly

Use the oral presentation rubric grid on page 12 as a guide to give up to 10 points. Mark these points under the extra category on the last page of each Unit Review in the student workbook.

Rubric for Essay Questions

	Beginning 1	Needs Improvement 2	Acceptable 3	Accomplished 4	Exemplary 5
Demonstrates Understanding of the topic	Student's work shows incomplete understanding of the topic	Student's work shows slight understanding of the topic	Student's work shows a basic understanding of the topic	Student's work shows complete understanding of the topic	Student's work demonstrates strong insight about the topic
Answered questions completely and accurately	Student's work did not address all of the questions	Student answered all of the questions with some accuracy	Student answered all questions with close to 100% accuracy	Student answered all questions with 100% accuracy	Student goes beyond the questions to demonstrate knowledge of the topic
Essay is neat and well organized	Student's work is sloppy and unorganized	Student's work is somewhat neat and organized	Student's essay is neat and somewhat organized	Student's work is well organized and neat	Student demonstrates extra care in organizing the essay and making it neat
Essay contains good grammar and spelling	Student's work is poorly written and hard to understand	Student's work contains some grammar, spelling and punctuation mistakes, but not enough to impede understanding	Student's work contains only 1 or 2 grammar, spelling or punctuation errors	Student's work contains no grammar, spelling or punctuation errors	Student's work is extremely well-written

Rubric for Oral Presentations

	Beginning 1	Needs Improvement 2	Acceptable 3	Accomplished 4	Exemplary 5
Preparation	Student did not prepare for the presentation	Student was somewhat prepared for the presentation	Student was prepared for the presentation and addressed the topic	Student was well-prepared for the presentation and addressed important points about the topic	Student prepared an excellent presentation that exhibited creativity and originality
Presentation Skills	Student demonstrated poor presentation skills (no eye contact, low volume, appears disinterested in the topic)	Student made some effort to demonstrate presentation skills (eye contact, spoke clearly, engaged audience, etc.)	Student demonstrated acceptable presentation skills (eye contact, spoke clearly, engaged audience, etc.)	Student demonstrated good presentation skills (eye contact, spoke clearly, engaged audience, etc.)	Student demonstrated strong presentation skills (eye contact, spoke clearly, engaged audience, etc.)

Rubric for Enrichment Activities

	Beginning 1	Needs Improvement 2	Acceptable 3	Accomplished 4	Exemplary 5
	Student's work is incomplete or inaccurate	Student's work is complete and somewhat inaccurate	Student completed the assignment with accuracy	Student's work is accurate, complete, neat and well-organized	Student demonstrates exceptional creativity or originality

UNIT 1: GLIMMERS OF GOLD

LESSON 1: BORDER HEATS UP

FACTS TO KNOW

Border – The geographical dividing line between two political or geographical entities

Survey – To examine and record an area's physical geography so one can create a border, map or plan

Thomas Riggs – Crew chief for the International Boundary Commission and governor of Alaska from 1918-1921

International Boundary Commission – The group in charge of keeping a visible border between two countries

COMPREHENSION QUESTIONS

1) Why was it a major problem that no border officially existed between Alaska and Canada in 1867?

There was no border in 1867, when the U.S. purchased Alaska from Russia for 2 cents an acre. And the lack of an agreed-upon boundary caused problems from the get-go. Maps of the time showed more land belonging to the Russians than was stipulated in an 1825 treaty between Russia and Great Britain. (Pages 8-9)

2) How did the Klondike Gold Rush cause an even greater need for a more defined border between Alaska and Canada around 1897?

When every square foot of ground could yield enormous wealth, the exact location of the border became critical. In fact, the total value of the gold mined in the Yukon was nearly $2.5 million in 1897 and almost $22.3 million in 1900. (Page 10)

3) Why did the stampeders disagree with the Canadians on the exact border?

Canadian officials wanted ownership of Skagway and Dyea, which would allow Canadians access to the Klondike gold fields without crossing American soil. Canada asserted that that location was more than 10 marine leagues from the sea, which was part of the 1825 boundary definition. But prospectors flooding into Skagway didn't agree. Americans thought that the head of Lake Bennett, another 12 miles north, should be the boundary between the two territories. (Pages 10-11)

4) How did the United States and Canada finally settle the border dispute in 1904?

A six-man tribunal was established to finally resolve the boundary issue in 1903. Roosevelt also sent word that if the panel did not settle the dispute to his liking, he would send in the U.S. Marines. The committee rejected the Canadian claims by a vote of four to two. The Alaska-Canada border was established on paper and various expeditions ordered to survey the vast area. (Pages 16-17)

5) How was the border marked? How long did it take to create the visible border?
In 1904, crews from both Canada and the United States started work on the panhandle of Southeast Alaska. They used boats, packhorses and backpacks to reach the remote mountains. A formal treaty was signed in 1908 between the United States and Great Britain setting up the International Boundary Commission to mark the boundary officially. It took Thomas Riggs and his crew eight summers to complete the job. (Pages 17-18)

DISCUSSION QUESTION

(Discuss this question with your teacher or write your answer in essay form below. Use additional paper if necessary.)

Describe the disagreement between Michael J. Heney and Stikine Bill Robinson.

_____

_____

_____

_____

_____

_____

_____

_____

_____

_____

_____

_____

_____

_____

_____

_____

_____

LEARN MORE

Look for this book in your local library:
Blazing Alaska's Trails. Brooks, Alfred H., Fairbanks: University of Alaska Press, 1953.

Map Activity

Using Page 16 of your textbook, trace the Alaska-Canada border onto the map below.
Mark the following towns: 1) Prince Rupert   2) Skagway   3) Juneau   4) Atlin

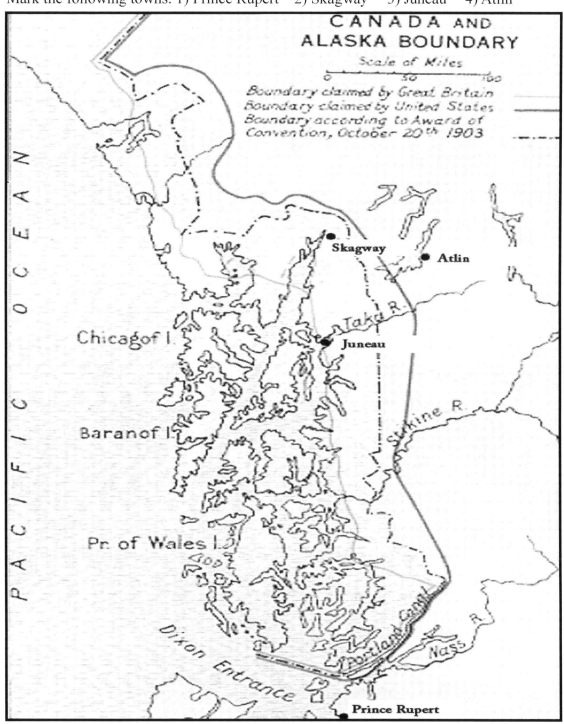

UNIT 1: GLIMMERS OF GOLD

LESSON 2: GOLD RUSH ENTERTAINERS ARRIVE

FACTS TO KNOW

Opera House – Dawson City's first theater
Vaudeville – Type of entertainment that is a mixture of comedy, song and dance
Monte Carlo – First theater in Dawson City to be powered by electricity
Palace Grand – One of Dawson City's largest theaters built by Arizona Charlie Meadows

COMPREHENSION QUESTIONS

1) Name two famous entertainers who performed in Nome? For what were they famous?
Sid Grauman, started his career producing tent shows in Nome. Alexander Pantages concluded that supplying amusement was sounder business than supplying supposedly primary needs. His Pantage's Orpheum provided the best show in town. Marjorie Rambeau was a great hit singing and playing a banjo at Tex Rickard's famous Northern Saloon in Nome. (Pages 20-21)

2) How did Dawson City become the largest city in Canada in 1898?
After the historic discovery of gold on Bonanza Creek in August 1896, Dawson City grew up from a marshy swamp near the confluence of the Yukon and Klondike rivers. In two years it had become the largest city in Canada west of Winnipeg with a population that fluctuated between 30,000 and 40,000 people. (Pages 23-24)

3) Describe Dawson's first opera house. What did it look like? What kind of performances did it showcase?
Dawson's first theater was grandiosely called the Opera House. It was in reality a log building with a bar and gambling rooms in front and a theater in the rear. "The programme was of a Vaudeville nature and included half a dozen song-and-dance 'artists,' a clog dancer, a wrestling match between Jim Slavin an old-time fighter, and Pat Rooney, a Canadian." (Pages 24-25)

4) What happened to the Opera House in 1897?
A masquerade ball was given in the Opera House on the evening before Thanksgiving 1897, and during the early hours of the following morning, the building caught fire. Before it could be checked, the building was totally destroyed. (Page 26)

5) Name three popular shows performed at the Palace Grand.
Local songs and sketches such as "Christmas on the Klondike," "The Klondike Millionaire" and "Star of the Yukon." Two outstanding hits were written and produced by John Milligan. Titled "Still Water Willie," and its sequel, "Still Water Willie's Wedding Night." Other locally written plays included a one-act "Ole Olson in the Klondike," and a full three-act comedy "Working a Lay in the Klondike." (Pages 27-28)

DISCUSSION QUESTION

(Discuss this question with your teacher or write your answer in essay form below. Use additional paper if necessary.)

Why do you think entertainment was such a big industry in places like Nome and Dawson City during the gold rushes?

_____
_____
_____
_____
_____
_____
_____
_____
_____
_____
_____
_____
_____
_____
_____
_____
_____

ENRICHMENT ACTIVITY

Listen to samples of Klondike Gold Rush music by visiting http://alaska-klondikemusic.com/

LEARN MORE

Look for this article at your local library:
"The Homes of Nome," in *The Alaska Journal* 4 (1) (Winter 1974): 17-20. Murtagh, William J.

UNIT 1: GLIMMERS OF GOLD

LESSON 3: GOLDEN HEART CITY GROWS

FACTS TO KNOW

Elbridge Truman Barnette – Called E.T., Barnette is credited with establishing Fairbanks in Alaska's interior

James Wickersham – District judge in Alaska who saw value in Fairbanks and moved his offices there in 1903

Felix Pedro – Italian prospector who discovered gold in the Tanana Valley

COMPREHENSION QUESTIONS

1) What led E.T. Barnette to start a trading post along the Chena River? What happened when he first set out to bring supplies to Alaska's interior?

Barnette thought a trading post sitting at a strategic spot with heavy traffic could make him a rich man, and a trading operation at Tanacross would be accessible by river in the summer and by railroad year-round. He decided to take a stock of supplies by steamship to St. Michael, transfer the goods onto a smaller boat and travel up the Yukon. While cruising around St. Michael harbor, his riverboat Arctic Boy hit a rock and sank. (Pages 35-37)

2) How did Barnette eventually start his trading post? Why did he name the spot Fairbanks?

Barnette asked Charles W. Adams, captain of the 150-foot steamer Lavelle Young, to get him as close to Tanacross as possible. Once the Captain got them as far as he thought he could go, the crew helped Barnette and his men build a small cabin and 6-foot-high walls for a 26-by-54-foot warehouse. Wickersham, the newly appointed U.S. district judge for the territory, suggested Barnette rename his post in honor of a man the judge mightily admired: Republican Sen. Charles W. Fairbanks of Indiana. (Pages 37-39)

3) How long did it take Felix Pedro to find gold in the Tanana Valley? How many claims had he staked by 1903?

Felix Pedro had discovered a large quantity of gold on a small, unnamed creek 12 miles north of Barnette's trading post. Pedro searched for gold in the Tanana Valley for seven years. After his rich discovery on July 22, he continued prospecting and by 1903 had interest in more than 12 claims in top-producing grounds. (Page 43)

4) How did E.T. Barnette promote the Fairbanks gold rush? How did the stampede later become a problem for him?

Barnette knew the potential for an all-out stampede to Alaska's Interior. He vigorously promoted the Tanana gold fields and even sent his cook, a Japanese musher named Jujiro Wada, to Dawson to spread the word. Barnette's promotion plan worked and soon he ran short of supplies. During the initial days, he had to hire men with rifles to guard his stock.

His high prices were a problem, too, and the miners finally retaliated. They held a miners' meeting and forced Barnette to cut his price on flour from $12 to $6 per sack. (Page 44)

5) When Judge Wickersham decided to move his judicial headquarters from Eagle to Fairbanks, how did that affect the population of the Interior town? What was his impression of Fairbanks as recorded in his diary in 1903?

Fairbanks had a reputation of being a lawless place. When Judge Wickersham built a jail and government offices at Third and Cushman streets, more people moved in. In his diary he wrote: "There are three streets roughly staked out through the woods, parallel to the river. There are probably 500 people here – mostly in tents, but log houses are being constructed as rapidly as possible. The town is just now in its formation period – town lots are at a premium – jumping, staking, recording, building." Wickersham's decision to move his judicial headquarters from Eagle to Fairbanks helped to clean up the town and make it the center of gold mining in the Interior. (Pages 56-57)

6) As the city of Fairbanks grew, what important transportation system materialized?

Residents of the area saw a need for dependable, year-round means of transportation to move people and supplies to and from the mines. The newly established Tanana Valley Railroad provided much-needed transportation to and from small communities it served. (Pages 59-60)

DISCUSSION QUESTION

(Discuss this question with your teacher or write your answer in essay form below. Use additional paper if necessary.)

What did Elbridge Barnette do after he sold two-thirds of his interest in the trading post to Northern Commercial Company? Why did this sale benefit Fairbanks? (Page 60)

_____
_____
_____
_____
_____
_____
_____
_____
_____
_____
_____
_____
_____
_____
_____
_____
_____

ENRICHMENT ACTIVITY

Imagine that you, like Elbridge Barnette, are establishing a new trading post in a high traffic area of Alaska during the gold rush. Write a journal entry about your exciting adventures. What is the area like? Who did you meet? What challenges did you face?

LEARN MORE

Look for these books at your local library:
E.T. Barnette: The Strange Story of the Man Who Founded Fairbanks, Terrance Cole. Anchorage: Alaska Northwest Publishing Company, 1981.

Frontier Politics: Alaska's James Wickersham. Atwood, Evangeline. Portland, Oregon: Binford & Mort, 1979.

TIME TO REVIEW

Review Chapters 1-3 of your book before moving on to the Unit Review. See how many questions you can answer without looking at your book.

Courtesy Alaska State Library

This April 1903 view of E.T. Barnette's trading post, known as Barnette's Cache, shows that Barnette and his crew had built a warehouse, far left, cabin and had started building a store. A few months later, Barnette received word that Felix Pedro had found large quantities of gold. The town of Fairbanks soon would rise around this trading post.

UNIT 1: GLIMMERS OF GOLD

REVIEW LESSONS 1-3

Write down what you remember about:

Border – _The geographical dividing line between two political or geographical entities_

Survey – _To examine and record an area's physical geography so one can create a border, map or plan_

Thomas Riggs – _Crew chief for the International Boundary Commission and governor of Alaska from 1918-1921_

International Boundary Commission – _The group in charge of keeping a visible border between two countries_

Opera House – _Dawson City's first theater_

Vaudeville – _Type of entertainment that is a mixture of comedy, song and dance_

Monte Carlo – _First theater in Dawson City to be powered by electricity_

Palace Grand – _One of Dawson City's largest theaters built by Arizona Charlie Meadows_

Elbridge Truman (E.T.) Barnette – _Credited with establishing Fairbanks in Alaska's interior_

James Wickersham – _District judge in Alaska who saw value in Fairbanks and moved his offices there in 1903_

Felix Pedro – _Italian prospector who discovered gold in the Tanana Valley_

Fill in the blanks.

1) Alaska's border with _Canada_ is one of the great feats of wilderness _surveying_. Marked by _metal cones_ and a _clear-cut swath_ 20 feet wide, the boundary is _1,538_ miles long.

2) _Canadian_ officials wanted ownership of _Skagway_ and _Dyea_, which would allow _Canadians_ access to the _Klondike_ gold fields without crossing _American_ soil. But _prospectors_ flooding into Skagway didn't agree. _Americans_ thought that the head of Lake Bennett, another 12 miles north, should be the boundary between the two territories.

3) A _six-man tribunal_ was established to finally resolve the boundary issue in _1903_. The _United States_ claimed a continuous stretch of coastline, unbroken by the deep fiords of the region. _Canada_ demanded control of the heads of certain fiords, especially the _Lynn_ Canal, as it gave access to the _Yukon_ River.

4) A formal treaty was signed in 1908 between the _United States_ and _Great Britain_ setting up the _International Boundary Commission_ to mark the boundary officially.

5) When Circle City and Fortymile were emptied as a result of the _Klondike gold strike_, _Dawson_ City became the center of entertainment. After the historic discovery of gold on _Rabbit (Bonanza)_ Creek in August _1896_, _Dawson_ City grew up from a marshy swamp near the confluence of the _Yukon_ and _Klondike_ rivers.

6) Dawson's first theater was grandiosely called the _Opera House_. It was in reality a _log_ building with a bar and gambling rooms in front and a theater in the rear. One of Dawson's finest theaters, The _Palace Grand_, was built by Arizona Charlie Meadows.

7) What kind of entertainment was offered to the patrons? Some examples include: _Songs and dances, comic sketches, one-act farces, local songs and sketches, and local plays._

8) _Fairbanks_, located on the _Chena_ River in Interior Alaska, didn't begin as a well-thought-out plan for civilization. It began as a wilderness _trading post_ set up in the wrong place at the wrong time of year.

9) *Elbridge "E.T." Barnette* thought a trading post sitting at a strategic spot with heavy traffic just might make him a rich man, and a trading operation at *Tanacross* would be accessible by river in the summer and by *railroad* year-round.

10) After hearing about the trading post along the *Chena* River, *James Wickersham*, the newly appointed U.S. district judge for the territory, suggested Barnette name his post in honor of a man the judge mightily admired: Republican Sen. Charles W. *Fairbanks* of Indiana.

Courtesy Alaska State Library

This photo of men surveying the Canada-Alaska border between 1907-1913 shows surveyors marking the line between the two countries somewhere around Mount St. Elias.

Notice the headgear the man sitting on the ground is wearing. Mosquitoes and biting gnats were a constant problem in the wilderness.

Glimmers of Gold
Crossword Puzzle

Read Across and Down clues and fill in blank boxes that match numbers on the clues

Across

3   E.T. Barnette sent him to Dawson to spread the word of the Fairbanks gold strike
8   The first theater in Dawson
11 To examine and record an area's physical geography so one can create a border/map
12 Barnette's riverboat that sank in St. Michael in the summer of 1901
14 The Golden Heart City
16 Judge who moved his judicial headquarters from Eagle to Nome
17 What E.T. Barnette first called his new settlement in Alaska's Interior
19 When ice melts and leaves rivers in the spring
22 A settlement that explodes with population in a short time due to something like a gold rush
25 These creatures swarmed Barnette and his group as they chopped down trees to clear space for his trading post
26 Name of Barnette's trading post
27 The country that rules Canada
30 City that grew up on a swampy marsh after gold was discovered on Bonanza Creek
31 A varied mixture of people or things like songs
34 The valley where the Fairbanks gold strike occurred
35 This was the mode of transportation between some of the mines near Fairbanks
36 This gold rush brought stampeders into the area that became Dawson
37 Crew chief for the International Boundary Commission
38 The geographical dividing line between two political or geographical entities
39 Some people thought this animal, named Wise Mike, was the most talented actor in Dawson
40 Owner of the Chinese Theatre in Hollywood

Down

1   Man who envisioned a settlement on the belief merchants in gold camps prospered more than miners
2   One of the biggest dangers to a gold-rush town
4   First theater in Dawson to be lit by electricity
5   A group of entertainers who travel and perform together
6   Country that borders Alaska
7   He played piano in the Northern Saloon in Nome when he was 8 years old
9   This theater was built by Arizona Charlie Meadows
10 Place where E.T. Barnette originally wanted to build a trading post
11 The con man that organized criminal activities along the railroad route from Southeast Alaska into Canada along the White Pass Trail
13 River along which the town of Fairbanks grew
15 Name of shallow-draft boat that E .T. Barnette had made in St. Michael
18 Places where gold is dug out of the ground
20 Depart quickly, hurry away
21 The man who found gold in sufficient quantity in 1902 that it drew people into Alaska's interior

Glimmers of Gold
Crossword Puzzle Key

Down (Continued)

23 Number of streets staked out through the woods in Fairbanks when Wickersham arrived in April 1903
24 Variety show of comedy, singing and dancing offered in Dawson City
25 A drawing of an area of land showing physical features, cities, roads, etc.
27 Type of gun Canadians mounted on the summits of Chilkoot and White passes during border dispute
28 Felix Pedro's mining companion
29 Captain that dropped E .T. Barnette and his supplies off along the Chena River
32 The canal in southeast Alaska that both the Americans and Canadians wanted control over
33 One of Broadway's leading beauties

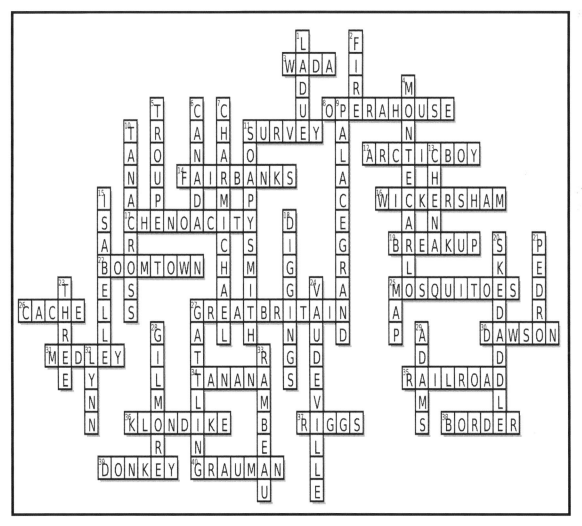

UNIT 1: GLIMMERS OF GOLD

UNIT TEST

Choose *two* of the following questions to answer in paragraph form. Use as much detail as possible to completely answer the question.

1) Why was it so important to establish an exact Alaska-Canada border? What was the dispute between Canada and the United States? How was the dispute resolved?

2) What was gold-rush entertainment like in places like Nome, Circle City and Dawson? What kind of performers were popular? Describe two famous places of entertainment you read about in Chapter 2.

3) Describe Elbridge Barnette's journey to establish the city of Fairbanks. Why did he set out to the Interior? What obstacles did he face? Why did he name the trading post Fairbanks?

TEACHER NOTES ABOUT THIS UNIT

UNIT 2: CROOKS RUN RAMPANT

LESSON 4: BLUE PARKA BANDIT STRIKES AGAIN
LESSON 5: TURN-OF-THE-CENTURY JUSTICE

Note: Read both chapters 4 and 5 before completing this lesson.

FACTS TO KNOW

Blue Parka Bandit – A notorious robber who preyed on the miners in Fairbanks
Hendrickson – Identity of the Blue Parka Bandit
Thornton – A horse thief that was a prisoner on the *Lavelle Young* with Hendrickson
Miners' Code – The law of the land in gold rush camps

COMPREHENSION QUESTIONS

1) Who was the last person robbed by the Blue Parka Bandit? What happened when the Blue Parka Bandit tried to rob him?
Bishop Peter Trimble Rowe, a popular Episcopalian missionary, was the last person robbed by the Blue Parka Bandit. The Bishop said to him, "Friend, is this the way you treat a minister of the gospel?" The Blue Parka Bandit asked if he was a minister. The Bishop told him who he was and the Bandit told him that he wouldn't rob him. The Bandit said that he was a member of the Bishop's church. (Pages 68-69)

2) How did law enforcement figure out the identity of the Blue Parka Bandit?
His robbing days came to an end when people noticed that a man named Hendrickson, a fugitive from prison, always seemed to be in the vicinity of the holdups. When various circumstances connected him with the robberies, Hendrickson was captured and jailed. (Pages 70-71)

3) What precautions did the guards aboard the *Lavelle Young* take to prevent the prisoners from escaping? How did they escape?
Hendrickson and Thornton had "Oregon Boots" attached to their shoes – circular disks of iron that weighed 30 pounds and clamped around the men's ankles by means of an inside hinge. These were secured by bolts sunk in small sockets, locked by screwing them tightly with a key. Hendrickson broke himself and his companions out of the Oregon Boots by sneaking a metal file in his pipe. They cut a hole into the ceiling using hooks. (Pages 73-77)

4) How did Hendrickson and Thornton get caught?
Hendrickson tried to hijack the boat of an ex-sheriff from Montana, who had a gun and was able to capture Hendrickson. Thornton turned himself in after he saw the marshal coming up the river. (Page 79)

5) Explain how the miners' code worked. How were disputes handled? How were guilty parties punished?

Each camp decided matters of common concern by majority vote and meted out justice to fit the crime. When a situation came along that necessitated a meeting, the miners came together and elected a judge and a sheriff. Defendants and plaintiffs then gave their sides of the story. After all the evidence was weighed, the miners would render a verdict: Murder was punished by hanging; stealing meant a sound whipping or banishment. The guilty had no notice of appeal, no bill of exceptions and no stay of execution. (Pages 80-81)

6) How were people married in gold rush camps when there were no judges or ministers?

With no judges or ministers, the miners had to come up with creative ways to perform nuptials. The miners wrote up their own marriage contracts and performed the ceremonies themselves. (Page 81)

DISCUSSION QUESTION

(Discuss this question with your teacher or write your answer in essay form below. Use additional paper if necessary.)

What do you think your hometown would be like if it were run by the miners' code? Do you think there would be more or less crime? Explain your answer.

_____
_____
_____
_____
_____
_____
_____
_____
_____
_____

ENRICHMENT ACTIVITY

Imagine that you are a miner in Nome during the gold rush era, and your camp put you in charge of writing the miners' code for your camp. How would you settle disputes? Who decides if someone is innocent or guilty? What punishments will you put into place? Is there an appeals process?

LEARN MORE

Look for this book at your local library:

The Alaskan Gold Fields. By Dunham, Sam C., Anchorage: Alaska Northwest Publishing Company, 1984. Book insert in THE ALASKA JOURNAL 14 (1) (Winter 1984).

UNIT 2: CROOKS RUN RAMPANT

LESSON 6: TOMBSTONE TEMPORARILY TRANSPLANTED

FACTS TO KNOW

Ed Schieffelin – A prospector from Arizona who searched for a highway of gold
Wyatt Earp – Infamous participant in the shootout at OK Corral
Tombstone – Historic city in Arizona where the OK Corral is located
Dexter Saloon – Wyatt Earp's "Second Class Saloon" in Nome

COMPREHENSION QUESTIONS

1) Where did Ed Schieffelin find silver before coming to Alaska? How long did he search?
Before arriving in Alaska in the 1880s, Schieffelin had searched for the mother lode of silver in the Apache country of Arizona. He searched for more than a decade before finding silver. (Pages 82-83)

2) What was his theory about finding gold in the Yukon? Was his prospecting trip successful? What happened?
He had an interesting theory that somewhere in Alaska a golden highway crossed the Yukon – a continuation of a great mineral belt that girdled the world from Cape Horn to Asia. Accustomed to the heat of Arizona, he became discouraged by the arctic bleakness and cold. He decided that mining in Alaska wouldn't pay. He sold his boat to pioneer explorers and traders Arthur Harper and Jack McQuesten, and for many years it was their lifeline to the outside world. (Pages 82-83)

3) What happened in the shootout at the OK Corral?
Virgil Earp, a U.S. marshal, had deputized his brothers, Wyatt and Morgan. They faced off with the Clanton gang, and when the bullets stopped flying, three members of the Clanton gang lay dead, and Virgil and Morgan Earp were wounded. The surviving Clantons charged that the Earp brothers and their friend, Doc Holliday, stalked their victims, some of whom were unarmed, and shot first without provocation. But the Earps and Holliday claimed that the Clantons were waiting for them and cocked their pistols first. (Pages 84-85)

4) What brought Wyatt Earp to Nome? What did he do there?
Wyatt Earp and his partner, Josie, went whenever a new gold-, silver- or copper-mining boomtown appeared. They invested in mines and real estate and operated saloons and gambling parlors, which eventually brought them to Alaska. Earp had fled Arizona

because he was under indictment for murder. He opened a saloon in Nome called Dexter Saloon. (Pages 85-86)

5) Why did Wyatt Earp go back to California during the winter? When did he leave Alaska for good?
Earp remained in Alaska for four years, running his business during the "season" for making money in mining districts in Alaska – late spring to early fall. When the ground started to freeze, he and Josie would head by steamer back to California because, as with most mining towns, Nome basically shut down. (Page 88)

DISCUSSION QUESTION

(Discuss this question with your teacher or write your answer in essay form below. Use additional paper if necessary.)

Stories like Wyatt Earp have been made into exciting movies. If you were a movie maker, what part of history would you like to turn into a movie? Why?

_____
_____
_____
_____
_____
_____
_____
_____
_____
_____
_____
_____
_____
_____
_____

ENRICHMENT ACTIVITY

Read more about Wyatt Earp by visiting https://www.britannica.com/biography/Wyatt-Earp or http://www.pbs.org/wgbh/americanexperience/features/timeline/wyatt/
Write a paragraph about what you learned.

LEARN MORE

Learn more about Nome by visiting: http://www.akhistorycourse.org/americas-territory/travel-travelers-agree-that-nomes-golden-lining-is-in-its-history

UNIT 2: CROOKS RUN RAMPANT

REVIEW LESSONS 4-6

Write down what you remember about:

Blue Parka Bandit – *A notorious robber who preyed on the miners in Fairbanks*

Hendrickson – *The robber who turned out to be the Blue Parka Bandit*

Thornton – *A horse thief that was a prisoner on the Lavelle Young with Hendrickson*

Miners' Code – *The law of the land in gold rush camps*

Ed Schieffelin – *A prospector from Arizona who searched for a highway of gold in Alaska*

Wyatt Earp – *Infamous participant in the shootout at OK Corral*

Tombstone – *Historic city in Arizona where the OK Corral is located*

Dexter Saloon – *Wyatt Earp's "Second Class Saloon" in Nome*

Fill in the blanks:

1) The *Blue Parka Bandit* had struck again. Alaskans felt they had a good joke on *Bishop Peter Trimble Rowe*, a popular Episcopalian missionary who was in the last party robbed by the daring highwayman.

2) When the citizens of Fairbanks saw the *Blue Parka Bandit* and *Thornton* board the *Lavelle Young* under the watchful eye of a federal marshal, they breathed a collective sigh of relief that the two wouldn't be in their town jail another winter.

3) The dinner gong sounded at 5:30 p.m. on October 6 while the _Lavelle Young_ and _Seattle No. 3_ were tied up at the _Nation_ City wood yard to take on fuel. A guard burst through the door and announced that The _Blue Parka Bandit_ had escaped.

4) Hendrickson engineered the escape. Somehow, he'd obtained a _broken piece of jeweler's file_ before leaving _Fairbanks_. He divided a brass tube into two pieces and used one as a key to unscrew the bolts locking the 30-pound _Oregon Boots_ on their feet.

5) A practical application of frontier democracy called the _miners' code_ was the only law that ruled the Far North. Each _camp_ decided matters of common concern by _majority vote._

6) After all the _evidence_ was weighed, the _miners_ would render a verdict: Murder was punished by _hanging_; stealing meant a sound _whipping_ or _banishment_. The guilty had no notice of _appeal,_ no bill of exceptions and no _stay of execution_.

7) After searching for more than a decade, _Ed Schieffelin_ finally discovered silver in the state of _Arizona_. Following his discovery, he founded the _Tombstone_ Mining District, which evolved into _Tombstone, Arizona_.

8) When the silver dwindled, _Schieffelin_ was determined to repeat his success with _gold_ in Alaska. He had an interesting theory that somewhere in Alaska a _golden highway_ crossed the Yukon – a continuation of a great mineral belt that girdled the world from Cape Horn to Asia.

9) _Wyatt Earp_ fled Arizona to go to _Nome_ because he was under suspicion for murder following the notorious 1881 massacre of _the Clantons_ at the _OK Corral_ and later the shooting of Frank Stillwell.

10) There were conflicting reports of what happened during the famous shootout at _OK Corral_. The surviving _Clantons_ charged that the _Earp_ brothers and their friend, _Doc Holliday_, stalked their victims, some of whom were unarmed, and shot first without provocation. But the _Earps_ and _Holiday_ claimed that the _Clantons_ were waiting for them and cocked their pistols first.

11) According to a letter found in the basement of the Juneau federal jail, _Wyatt Earp_ wanted to settle down in _Juneau._ But a posse met his ship and told him _that he was not welcome there._

12) After _Wyatt Earp_ arrived in Nome, he built the _Dexter_ saloon and billed it as _the only second class saloon in Alaska._

13) After _Wyatt Earp_ and his partner, _Josie,_ left Nome for good, they lived in California where he spent years writing _his autobiography_ and _a screenplay based on his career as a lawman._

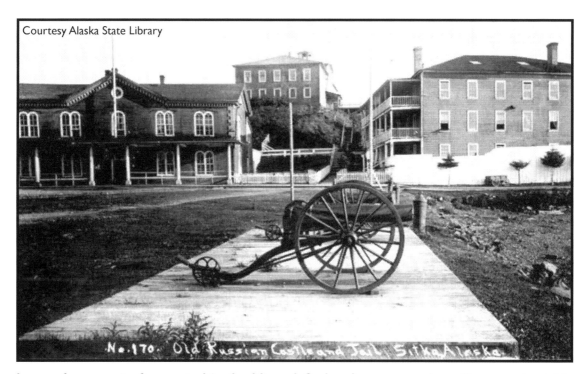

Courtesy Alaska State Library

No. 170. Old Russian Castle and Jail, Sitka Alaska.

Law enforcement often rested in the Miners' Code when prospectors discovered gold in the Klondike region, Nome and Fairbanks. But as this photograph taken in Sitka shows, a jail – along with the Baranof Castle, Marine barracks and custom house – was built by the Russians after they settled in Southeast Alaska in the early 1800s. The Russians brought their brand of justice with them when they colonized parts of Alaska, and the U.S. War Department carried out laws following the Alaska purchase in 1867.

Early Law and Order
Word Search Key
Find the words listed below

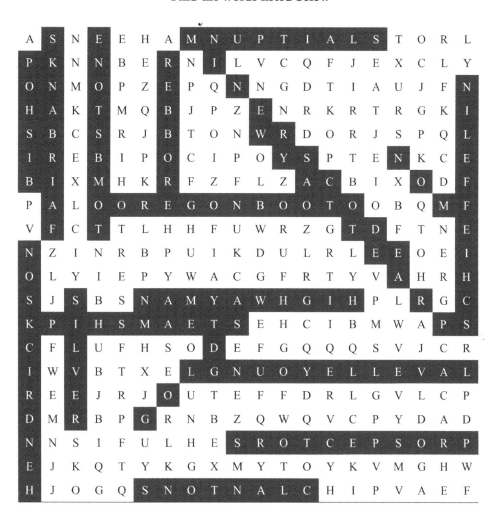

A	S	N	E	E	H	A	M	N	U	P	T	I	A	L	S	T	O	R	L
P	K	N	N	B	E	R	N	I	L	V	C	Q	F	J	E	X	C	L	Y
O	N	M	O	P	Z	E	P	Q	N	N	G	D	T	I	A	U	J	F	N
H	A	K	T	M	Q	B	J	P	Z	E	N	R	K	R	T	R	G	K	I
S	B	C	S	R	J	B	T	O	N	W	R	D	O	R	J	S	P	Q	L
I	R	E	B	I	P	O	C	I	P	O	Y	S	P	T	E	N	K	C	E
B	I	X	M	H	K	R	F	Z	F	L	Z	A	C	B	I	X	O	D	F
P	A	L	O	O	R	E	G	O	N	B	O	O	T	O	O	B	Q	M	F
V	F	C	T	T	L	H	H	F	U	W	R	Z	G	T	D	F	T	N	E
N	Z	I	N	R	B	P	U	I	K	D	U	L	R	L	E	E	O	E	I
O	L	Y	I	E	P	Y	W	A	C	G	F	R	T	Y	V	A	H	R	H
S	J	S	B	S	N	A	M	Y	A	W	H	G	I	H	P	L	R	G	C
K	P	I	H	S	M	A	E	T	S	E	H	C	I	B	M	W	A	P	S
C	F	L	U	F	H	S	O	D	E	F	G	Q	Q	Q	S	V	J	C	R
I	W	V	B	T	X	E	L	G	N	U	O	Y	E	L	L	E	V	A	L
R	E	E	J	R	J	O	U	T	E	F	F	D	R	L	G	V	L	C	P
D	M	R	B	P	G	R	N	B	Z	Q	W	Q	V	C	P	Y	D	A	D
N	N	S	I	F	U	L	H	E	S	R	O	T	C	E	P	S	O	R	P
E	J	K	Q	T	Y	K	G	X	M	Y	T	O	Y	K	V	M	G	H	W
H	J	O	G	Q	S	N	O	T	N	A	L	C	H	I	P	V	A	E	F

HENDRICKSON	HIGHWAYMAN	ROBBER
FAIRBANKS	BISHOP	PROSPECTORS
OREGON BOOT	LAVELLE YOUNG	MINERS CODE
NUPTIALS	TOMBSTONE	WYATT EARP
SCHIEFFELIN	STEAMSHIP	CLANTONS
SILVER	GOLD	NOME

UNIT 2: CROOKS RUN RAMPANT

UNIT TEST

Choose *two* of the following questions to answer in paragraph form. Use as much detail as possible to completely answer the question.

1) Describe what happened on the *Lavelle Young* on October 6, 1905.

2) How did the miners' code work? Who made decisions? How were guilty parties punished?

3) Who was Ed Schieffelin? Where was he from? What was his theory about gold in Alaska? Did he prove his theory to be true?

4) What happened at the O.K. Corral in Tombstone? Who was involved? What were the conflicting accounts?

_____

_____

_____

_____

_____

_____

_____

_____

_____

_____

_____

_____

_____

_____

_____

_____

_____

_____

_____

_____

TEACHER NOTES ABOUT THIS UNIT

UNIT 3: LAW AND ORDER

LESSON 7: ALASKA'S FIRST LAWMEN

FACTS TO KNOW

Frank Canton – First lawman in Alaska's interior

Lawman – A person in charge of enforcing the law

Capt. Michael Healy – First U.S. Revenue Marine cutter commander to make regular patrols into harsh arctic waters

Revenue Cutter – A sea vessel used to enforce federal law under the U.S. Revenue Marine branch

COMPREHENSION QUESTIONS

1) How did Frank Canton become the first lawman in Alaska's interior?

Portus B. Weare, a leading shareholder of the North American Transportation and Trading Company, which was challenging the monopoly of the Alaska Commercial Company, felt his business needed the protection of a vigorous law enforcement officer. Weare agreed to supplement Canton's $750 a year salary. (Pages 90-91)

2) What happened on his way to Circle City?

On his way to his new post, weather forced Canton to spend the winter in Rampart in 1898. He tried prospecting, but heard about a steamboat near Rampart where the passengers mutinied against their captain. He hiked to the vessel, arrested the leaders and held a trial with the other passengers. Canton recognized one of the leaders as a fugitive from Idaho with a $2,500 bounty on his head. Canton arrested him, and as soon as the ice went out on the Yukon River, he hauled the fellow to Circle City. (Pages 91-92)

3) Why was it difficult for him to do his job when he got to Circle City?

By the time he reached his post, many of the stampeders had left for Dawson. Their exodus meant that city coffers were limited, so the lawman had no funds with which to operate. He also found that no one in the community wanted to board federal prisoners for $3 a day, nor act as jailers. Canton had to borrow money to run his office. (Page 92)

4) Why was Frank Canton discharged as deputy? What was revealed after his death?

He was discharged when officials learned he had resigned his Oklahoma position while being audited for fraudulent expense claims. Following his death, it was revealed that his real name was Joe Horner, a wanted outlaw, murderer and bank robber who started out as a badman in Texas and later changed his name. (Pages 92-94)

5) How did Michael Healy enforce the law?

Capt. Michael A. Healy was about the only source of law in a lawless land, and he transported criminals onboard the cutter Bear from remote Alaska communities to Sitka for trial. He had a reputation for being a strict commander and at times even cruel. (Pages 96-101)

6) In what other ways did Healy serve the people of Alaska?

At his own expense, Healy transported 16 reindeer from the Natives of the Siberian Coast to the Seward Peninsula. In 1892, another 171 reindeer were added to the herd and Teller Reindeer Station was established. More reindeer followed. These selfless acts and humanitarian efforts helped Natives continue their subsistence ways and probably saved many lives. (Page 98)

DISCUSSION QUESTION

(Discuss this question with your teacher or write your answer in essay form below. Use additional paper if necessary.)

What challenges did Alaska's early lawmen face?

_____

_____

_____

_____

_____

_____

_____

_____

_____

_____

ENRICHMENT ACTIVITY

Although Michael Healy was honored for all the good that he did, we read about two accounts of him treating people badly aboard his ship. History is full of people that we remember for the great things they did, but they did some bad things, too. Can you think of one example? If not, do some research at the library or online. Write a paragraph or two about both the good and bad things that this person did in his/her life. Conclude your writing with what that person is most remembered for doing.

LEARN MORE

Read more about Capt. Michael Healy and the U.S. Revenue cutter *Bear* by visiting http://www.akhistorycourse.org/northwest-and-arctic/1871-1897-arctic-explorations

UNIT 3: LAW AND ORDER

LESSON 8: JUDGE'S LIGHT SHINES ON

FACTS TO KNOW

Judge James Wickersham – One of the most influential figures in Alaska history

Traveling court – A group of jurors and other lawmen that traveled to decide a case where there were not enough people to summon sufficient jurors

Alfred Noyes – The corrupt judge in Nome who left mining disputes unsettled to take money for himself

Denali – Indian word for Mt. McKinley (Judge Wickersham was the first to organize a trip to climb Denali)

COMPREHENSION QUESTIONS

1) What new system did Judge James Wickersham begin in 1900? Why did he see a need for this? *Judge James Wickersham initiated a traveling judicial system. His system evolved after he sailed to Unalaska in 1900 to preside over the first felony trial on the Aleutian Chain. Recognizing that Unalaska's small population wouldn't allow him to summon sufficient jurors, he took more than a dozen people with him to Valdez and set up court in a building housing the town's laundry. (Page 104)*

2) It was said, jokingly, in the Northwest that *James Wickersham* was sent to Alaska to get him out of *Washington* politics. If so, *Washington* tossed a whole hornet's nest into Alaska, for he was the storm center of more *controversies* and is credited with having *written and made more history* than any other of Alaska's early public figures.

3) Describe the mess that Judge Wickersham was hired to clean up in Nome.
He went to Nome to clean up many unresolved mining claims. Alexander McKenzie had arranged to have President William McKinley appoint Alfred N. Noyes as judge of one of the three newly created judicial districts in Alaska. Judge Noyes put the claims into receiverships to be administered by McKenzie, who then hired men to mine the claims and commandeer all assets. (Pages 105-110)

4) According to his journal entries, how did Judge Wickersham resolve the mess in Nome? *Judge Wickersham dismissed many of the indictments against the miners. He said in his journal, "I am pleased to know that mine owners now express a feeling of safety over property rights and do me the honor to say that investments can now be made here with assurance of fair protection." (Page 110)*

5) Name at least two of the "firsts" attributed to Judge Wickersham.
He started the first traveling court in Alaska, the first court ever held in the Aleutians. He is credited with the first organized attempt to climb Mount McKinley. He published the first newspaper in Fairbanks and the Tanana Valley. In 1915, he brought together all the Native chiefs of Interior Alaska and organized the first Indian Council held in Fairbanks to discuss the effects of the railroad and homesteading on the Native way of life – one of the earliest considerations of Native land claims in Alaska. (Pages 113-114)

6) While serving Alaska, Wickersham found the Library of Congress had no Alaska section. What did he do about this?
He remedied the situation by preparing a bibliography of Alaska literature, amassing 10,380 items in his tremendous undertaking – perhaps the most gigantic historical task ever attempted by a single man. (Page 114)

DISCUSSION QUESTION

(Discuss this question with your teacher or write your answer in essay form below. Use additional paper if necessary.)

Why is Judge James Wickersham an important figure in Alaska's history?

_____
_____
_____
_____
_____
_____
_____
_____
_____
_____

ENRICHMENT ACTIVITY

Put together your own mini bibliography of Alaska history. Visit your local library or use your home computer to search for at least 5-10 books, Websites or magazine articles on Alaska history. Write down the title, author, date of publication, place of publication and publication company for each resource.

LEARN MORE

Look for this book at your local library:
Frontier Politics: Alaska's James Wickersham. By Evangeline Atwood. Portland, Oregon: Binford & Mort, 1979.

Early Alaska Lawmen
Crossword Puzzle

Read Across and Down clues and fill in blank boxes that match numbers on the clues

Across

3 To appease the anger or anxiety of someone
5 First U.S. Revenue cutter to regularly ply Alaska's waters in an effort to bring law and order
9 Keeping someone from harm
11 Wickersham moved to this new center of gold mining in 1903
15 First U. S. Revenue cutter commander to make regular patrols into harsh arctic waters
16 Town where Judge Wickersham held the first traveling court
21 She interpreted for the captain of the U.S. Revenue cutter *Bear*
22 The people of Fairbanks honored Judge Wickersham with this when their courthouse was dedicated on July 4, 1904
26 Name of crooked judge in Nome
27 An upright bar, post or frame forming a support or barrier used on U. S. Revenue cutters for disciplinary measures
29 To say that something may not be true
30 A formal charge or accusation of a serious crime
34 Another name for Mt. McKinley
35 Something that causes much discussion, disagreement or argument
38 The real name of the first lawman in Interior Alaska
39 Interior Alaska's first lawman was appointed as this (official title)
40 Where Interior Alaska's first lawman spent his first winter in 1898
41 Judge Wickersham produced one newspaper using this machine
42 Wickersham amassed 10,380 items of Alaska literature for this to be included in the Library of Congress
43 A light, fast coastal patrol boat
44 Not satisfied with something

Down

1 To haul up and lash securely
2 To confine someone as a punishment for a crime
4 Judge Wickersham's first official judicial headquarters was in this town
7 Small cord
8 Number of successive terms that Alaskans elected Judge Wickersham as their delegate to Congress
10 One who illegally occupies property to which another has a legal claim
12 Town in Southeast Alaska where prisoners from the Interior were taken for trial
13 U.S. Revenue cutters often served as these
14 Unrestrained by law
17 The people along the Siberian coast that raised reindeer
18 Planks, bars or logs where something heavy may be slid or rolled along
19 Relating to the government or public affairs of a country
20 An illegal or dishonest scheme for obtaining money

Early Alaska Lawmen
Crossword Puzzle Key

Down (Continued)

23 Those who work as sailors
24 Type of animals brought from Siberia to Alaska to help feed Natives and miners
25 Wickersham lived in this Alaska town until his death in 1939
28 A person who seeks to promote human welfare
31 Where Interior Alaska's first lawman was to set up his headquarters and build a jail
32 District judge of newly organized Third Judicial Division of Alaska
33 To clear someone of blame
36 First lawman in Interior Alaska
37 An application to a higher court for a decision to be reversed

UNIT 3: LAW AND ORDER

LESSON 9: *CITY OF SEATTLE* TURNS TO PIRACY
LESSON 10: INMATE NO. 594

Note: Read both chapters 9 and 10 before completing this lesson.

FACTS TO KNOW

Totem poles – Very large Native American sculptures mostly carved on logs that often tell a story or represent an event

City of Seattle – A steamship that carried a group from Seattle to Sitka to steal a totem pole

Robert Stroud – A miner who killed a man in Juneau and wrote books about birds and bird diseases while serving a life sentence

Alcatraz – A famous maximum security prison located on Alcatraz Island in the San Francisco Bay

COMPREHENSION QUESTIONS:

1) Why did the group from Seattle travel to Sitka to find a totem pole? What happened when they got there?
Those who carved totem poles only came from the tribes of northern Vancouver Island, the Queen Charlotte Islands and the adjacent tribes in British Columbia and Alaska. After finishing her business in the port of Sitka, the City of Seattle sailed out a bit and then anchored in a stream. Businessmen on board the ship rowed a small boat to the shore and chopped down a totem pole while Native villagers were away fishing. The crew chopped it in two to make it easier to carry. (Page 117)

2) Who did they steal the totem pole from? What did this group demand from the thieves? What did they receive in return?
The totem pole belonged to the Raven Clan of the Tlingit tribe. The Tlingits demanded $20,000 for the return of the stolen totem, but settled for $500, which the Seattle Post-Intelligencer paid. (Page 118)

3) Where was the totem pole kept after it was stolen? What happened to it in 1938?
On Oct. 18, 1899, the 60-foot totem was unveiled in Seattle's Pioneer Square. The original totem stood proudly in Pioneer Square until a careless smoker tossed a cigarette butt against its decaying base in 1938. The city removed the original totem and replaced it in 1940 with a replica carved by the descendants of the original totem's carvers. (Page 118)

4) Why was Robert Stroud sent to prison for seven years?

Robert Stroud pleaded guilty to a charge of second-degree murder. He was sentenced to serve seven years at the federal penitentiary on McNeil Island near Tacoma, Washington for shooting and killing Charles Damer in Juneau. (Page 122)

5) What did Robert Stroud do right before his release that caused him to be sentenced to death? How did his death sentence get changed to a life sentence in solitary confinement?

Just before the bartender's scheduled release on March 26, 1916, he walked into the Leavenworth mess hall and stabbed to death prison guard Andrew F. Turner. Robert Stroud's mother was able to talk to President Wilson's wife and begged her to save her son. Mrs. Wilson was impressed with the inmate's pioneer work with birds, and convinced her husband to commute the death sentence. (Pages 122-123)

6) What did Robert Stroud do while he served his sentence in Leavenworth? What was his nickname while imprisoned at Alcatraz?

He authored two books on canaries and their diseases, having raised nearly 300 birds in his cells, carefully studying their habits and physiology. He also wrote a manuscript called "Looking Outward" about prison reform that was never published. His nickname, "The Birdman of Alcatraz," came from his life on the rock. (Pages 123-124)

DISCUSSION QUESTION:

(Discuss this question with your teacher or write your answer in essay form below. Use additional paper if necessary.)

Do you think that the Tlingit people were properly compensated for the stolen totem pole? Explain your answer.

_____
_____
_____
_____
_____
_____
_____
_____
_____
_____
_____
_____
_____

ENRICHMENT ACTIVITY:

The totem pole that was stolen from the Raven Clan was craved in honor of a special woman called Chief-to-all-Women in 1790. Draw or paint your own totem pole either on a sheet of paper or on an empty paper towel roll. Present your totem pole or drawing to your class, and explain what it represents.

Read the link from the Learn More section for inspiration.

LEARN MORE:

Read more about how totem poles are made by visiting https://www.warpaths2peace-pipes.com/native-indian-art/how-to-make-a-totem-pole.htm

Southeast Alaska communities are home to many totem poles. Unfortunately many of the totems in Kake, such as those in this photo taken in the late 1890s, were destroyed when missionaries misunderstood their meanings and thought them idols created by the Native people.

UNIT 3: LAW AND ORDER

LESSON 11: ALASKA'S FIRST SERIAL KILLER

FACTS TO KNOW

Edward Krause – Alaska's first serial killer

Treadwell Gold Mining Company – At one time one of the largest gold mining companies in the world

Sequestered jury – When a judge orders that a jury be isolated from the public for the duration of a trial

COMPREHENSION QUESTIONS

1) Who first suspected that Edward Krause had something to do with the disappearance of James Christie? Why did they suspect Krause?
The Treadwell Mining Company hired the Pinkerton Detective Agency to investigate the disappearance of James Christie. When it was learned that Krause also was identified as the last person to see a missing charter boat operator out of Juneau, a warrant for his arrest was issued on charges of impersonating a federal officer. (Pages 126-127)

2) How did the police discover that Krause was responsible for more than one disappearance?
Krause escaped onboard a steamer heading for Seattle. A passenger recognized Krause from a wanted poster, and the police were alerted. A search of Krause's possessions turned up incriminating evidence, including forged documents, bank accounts and real estate transactions, which tied him to not only the recent disappearances in Juneau, but to the disappearances of at least eight other men, too. (Page 127)

3) What was uncovered about Edward Krause during the yearlong investigation?
After Krause was returned to Alaska, his true identity surfaced. Krause was really Edward Slompke, who'd served with the U. S. Army at Wrangell in 1897. The investigation revealed a series of disappearances and an intricate pattern of forged property transactions. Authorities found that over the years Krause recovered the assets of the murdered men. (Page 128)

4) Who were Edward Krause's supporters? What did they believe about Krause? Why were they dangerous? *The Western Federation of Miners labor movement thought that Edward Krause was being framed by Treadwell Mining Company. Undercover government agents discovered there were plans to get witnesses to change their testimony and threats to potential jurors. (Pages 127-128)*

5) What two firsts in Alaska court history occurred during the Edward Krause trials?
To protect the jury from intimidation by Krause's still-active supporters, the judge sequestered the jury during the trial – a first in Alaska court history. Krause's trial also marked the first extensive use in Alaska of testimony from handwriting and typewriter experts. (Page 128)

6) What was the verdict in the Krause case? What happened after sentencing?
The jury found Krause guilty of first-degree murder. His conviction was affirmed by the U.S. Court of Appeals in San Francisco, and Krause was sentenced to die by hanging at Juneau. He escaped federal prison two days before his scheduled execution. A reward was offered for him. A homesteader killed Krause after the fugitive stepped out of a stolen skiff onto the beach at Admiralty Island. (Page 129)

DISCUSSION QUESTION

(Discuss this question with your teacher or write your answer in essay form below. Use additional paper if necessary.)

"The true story of Krause's criminal enterprises and their extent will never be known. But if the story could ever be told, it would undoubtedly be one of the most startling in the annals of American crime history," stated a letter to the Department of Justice, written by attorney James Smiser of Juneau.

What did attorney Smiser mean by this statement? Why will the whole story never be told?

_____
_____
_____
_____
_____
_____
_____
_____
_____
_____
_____
_____

TIME TO REVIEW

Review Chapters 7-11 of your book before moving on to the Unit Review. See how many questions you can answer without looking at your book.

MAP ACTIVITY

Find the following places from Krause's story on the map below. Use the lesson for help, then write the name of each Southeast Alaska town in its proper box on the map.

1)   Juneau
2)   Petersburg
3)   Ketchikan
4)   Wrangell

Also locate 5) Sitka, the town from which a totem pole was stolen from the Raven Clan in the late 1890s.

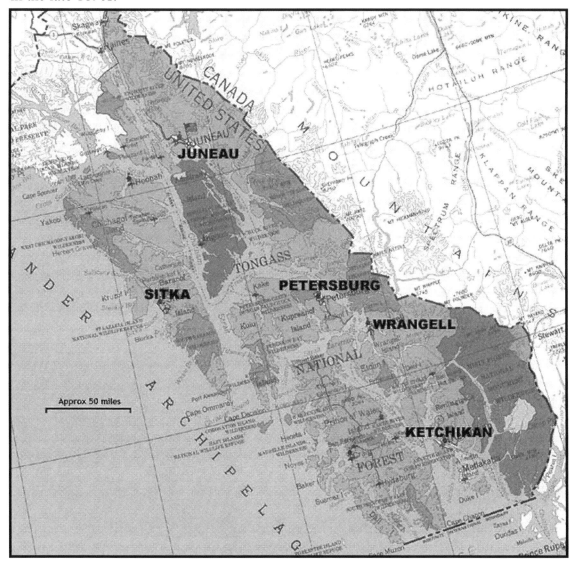

UNIT 3: LAW AND ORDER

REVIEW LESSONS 7-11

Write down what you remember about:

Frank Canton – _First lawman in Alaska's interior_

Lawman – _A person in charge of enforcing the law_

Capt. Michael Healy – _First U.S. Revenue Marine cutter commander to make regular patrols into harsh arctic waters_

Revenue Cutter – _A sea vessel used to enforce federal law under the U.S. Revenue Marine branch_

Judge James Wickersham – _One of the most influential figures in Alaska history_

Traveling court – _A group of jurors and other lawmen that travel to decide a case where there were not enough people to summon sufficient jurors_

Alfred Noyes – _The corrupt judge in Nome who left mining disputes unsettled to take money for himself_

Denali – _Native Alaskan word for Mount McKinley/Judge Wickersham was the first to organize a trip to climb Denali_

Totem pole – _Tall Native American sculptures mostly carved on logs that often tell a story or represent an event_

**City of Seattle** – _A steamship that carried a group from Seattle to Sitka to steal a totem pole_

Robert Stroud – _A miner who killed a man in Juneau and wrote monumental books about birds and bird diseases while serving a life sentence_

Alcatraz – _Famous maximum security prison on Alcatraz Island in the San Francisco Bay_

Edward Krause – _Alaska's first serial killer_

Treadwell Gold Mining Company – _At one time one of the largest gold mining companies in the world_

Sequestered jury – _When a judge orders that a jury be isolated from the public for the duration of a trial_

Fill in the blanks:

1) _Frank Canton_ found his work cut out for him when he headed to _Circle City_ to serve as the first lawman in Interior Alaska in the late 1890s.

2) By the time he reached his new post, _Canton_ found that most of the miners had moved on to _Dawson._ Their exodus meant that city coffers were limited, so the lawman had no _funds_ with which to operate. He also found that no one in the community wanted to board federal prisoners for $3 a day, nor act as jailers.

3) Life wasn't easy for Alaska's early lawmen. U.S. marshals didn't have _budgets_ to pursue, capture or hold evildoers who committed crimes in the territory. Due to the logistics of covering _such a large expanse of land_, suspects sometimes roamed at large for months, perhaps years, before being taken into custody. There was also the problem of transporting the prisoners to _Sitka_ for trial.

4) _Judge James Wickersham_ set up Alaska's first official _traveling_ court in the laundry building in _Valdez_ in 1900.

5) _Judge James Wickersham_ was called upon to travel to _Nome_ to clear up disputed _claims._ When _Alexander McKenzie_, an influential Republican, arranged to have President William McKinley appoint _Alfred Noyes_ as judge of one of three newly created judicial districts in Alaska, the stage was set to separate hardworking miners from their claims.

6) The steamer, _City of Seattle_, carried a delegation on board in 1899 that stole a _totem pole_ from the _Tlingit Indians_ in the city of _Sitka_, Alaska.

7) After murdering a man in _Juneau_ in 1909, _Robert Stroud_ was sentenced to _seven_ years in prison. Just before his scheduled release, he _stabbed a prison guard to death_ and was sentenced _to be hung_. His mother spoke to _Elizabeth Bolling Wilson_, who convinced her husband, _U.S. President Woodrow Wilson_, to change his sentence to solitary confinement for life.

8) His nickname, "*Birdman of Alcatraz,*" came from his life on the rock. And his monumental work, "*Stroud's Book of Bird Diseases,*" published in 1942, still is regarded as an authoritative source.

9) *Edward Krause* showed up at the *Treadwell* Mining Company and asked for a mine worker named *James Christie*, and that's the last time anyone ever saw the unfortunate miner.

10) To protect the jury from intimidation by Krause's still-active *supporters*, the judge *sequestered* the jury during the trial – a first in Alaska court history. Krause's trial also marked the first extensive use in Alaska of *testimony from handwriting and typewriter* experts.

Courtesy Alaska State Library

Law enforcement in Alaska was not a glamorous way of life, as this 1903 photo of the Ofice of the Deputy U.S. Marshal in Candle City shows.

Law and Order Southeast Alaska Style

Word Scramble Puzzle

Please unscramble the words below

1.	tmteo	totem	Item that people on board the City of Seattle stole from Southeast Alaska in 1899.
2.	nvera	raven	Clan of people in Sitka that demanded payment for their stolen property.
3.	rnoeeip	pioneer	Famous Seattle square where a Tlingit monument was placed in 1899.
4.	tuosdr	stroud	Last name of convict who wrote a research book on canaries
5.	acrlatza	alcatraz	Famous prison on a rocky island near San Francisco.
6.	woinls	wilson	U.S. president who commuted Birdman's sentence from death to life imprisonment.
7.	auerks	krause	Alaska's first serial killer.
8.	letlwreda	treadwell	Famous gold mine in Juneau.
9.	koptnneri	pinkerton	Well-known detective agency hired to investigate the disappearance of a man named Christie.
10.	mehotarsede	homesteader	Person who claimed the reward for the apprehension of Krause on Admiralty Island.

UNIT 3: LAW AND ORDER

UNIT TEST

Choose *three* of the following questions to answer in paragraph form. Use as much detail as possible to completely answer the question.

1) Name three challenges that early lawmen faced in Alaska.

2) What were three important things that Judge James Wickersham did while serving Alaska? Explain the significance of each one.

3) Why would some people call the *City of Seattle* a pirate ship? Describe what happened in 1899 when the steamship traveled to Sitka.

4) Who was the Birdman of Alcatraz? How did he earn this nickname? How did he end up in Alcatraz?

5) What was Edward Krause convicted of in 1917? How did he get caught? What two firsts in Alaska court history occurred during his trial?

TEACHER NOTES ABOUT THIS UNIT

UNIT 4: ROUTES TO RESOURCES

LESSON 12: ARIZONA EDITOR MAKES MARK ON ALASKA

FACTS TO KNOW

John Clum – Editor of the *Tombstone Epitaph* and the first appointed post office inspector for Alaska

Post Office Inspector – The person who regulates and oversees the post offices

COMPREHENSION QUESTIONS

1) Name three of John Clum's ventures. *He was the editor of the Tombstone Epitaph, the first mayor of Tombstone and the first post office inspector in Alaska. He dabbled in mining and politics, but was not successful at either. (Pages 131,136)*

2) Describe John Clum's duties as the post office inspector. Was this an easy job? Explain your answer. *John and his son, Woodworth, spent five months traveling 8,000 miles around Alaska and the Yukon setting up new post offices and equipping others. This was not an easy job. It was no job for a weakling – one of his inspection trips was made on "foot and in a snowstorm" to Chilkat, and a second trip, according to his diary, was via reindeer and "lap" sled. (Page 133)*

3) Use your book to fill in the blanks and follow John Clum's route to establish post offices throughout Alaska:

He established post offices in Southeast Alaska at *Sheep* Camp, the last station before the Chilkoot Pass, *Pyramid Harbor* and *Canyon*. Clum reestablished the post office at Haines and reorganized the offices at *Skagway* and *Dyea*.

Then he started down the Yukon River.

Clum and his son traveled to *Dawson*. From *Dawson*, he traveled to *Eagle* via *Fortymile*. At *Eagle*, he established the first new post office of the Interior, and then traveled 18 miles down the *Yukon* River to set up another post office at *Starr*, located at the mouth of Seventymile River.

His next stop was *Circle* City, where the first post office on the Yukon River had been established in 1896. He found the post office there, under Jack McQuesten, "in good order." On July 1, 1898, he and his son boarded the steamer *Seattle No. 1* for its maiden voyage down the Yukon to *St. Michael*, stopping to establish post offices at *Fort Yukon, Rampart, Weare, Koyukuk, Nulato and Anvik.*

DISCUSSION QUESTION

(Discuss this question with your teacher or write your answer in essay form below. Use additional paper if necessary.)

Why do you think mail service was so important to Alaskans during this time?

_____
_____
_____
_____
_____
_____
_____
_____
_____
_____
_____
_____
_____
_____
_____
_____

MAP ACTIVITY

There are three maps on the next two pages that show where John Clum traveled to set up new post offices in Alaska. The map on Page 54 shows the route he took in Southeast Alaska. The top map on Page 55 shows the route along the Yukon River and the bottom map shows Prince William Sound, Cook Inlet and the Aleutian Islands. See if you can mark on the maps the names of the towns where Clum established post offices.

LEARN MORE

Learn more about the start of the post office in Alaska by visiting http://www.akhistory-course.org/americas-territory/alaskas-heritage/chapter-4-13-communications

Mark the following settlements where John Clum founded new post offices along the Chilkoot Trail in Southeast Alaska:
 1) Dyea   2) Canyon   3) Sheep Creek

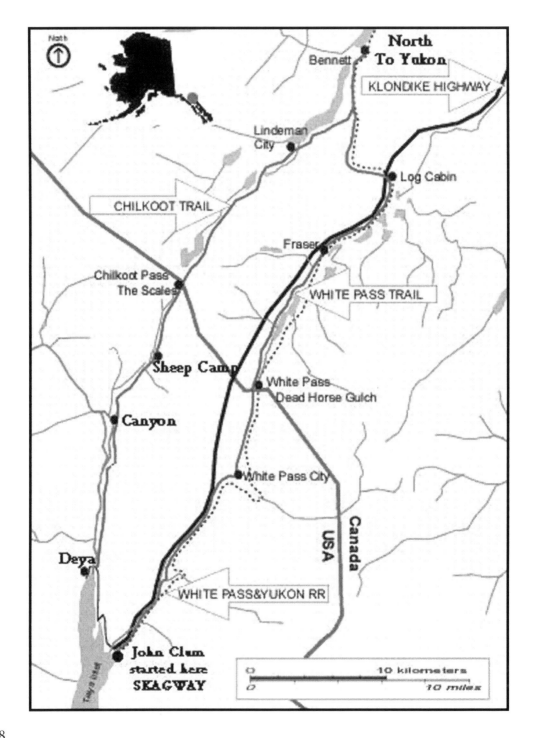

Mark the following settlements where John Clum founded new post offices along the Yukon River: 1) Eagle 2) Fort Yukon 3) Rampart 4) Koyukuk 5) Nulato 6) Anvik

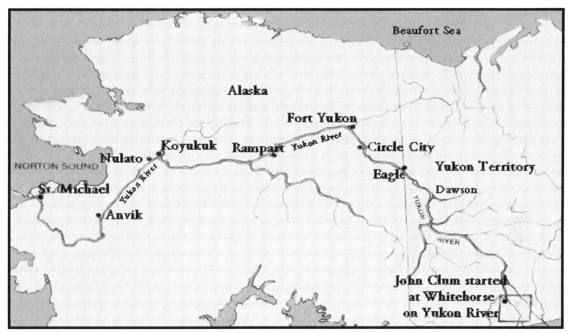

Mark the following settlements where John Clum founded new post offices in Cook Inlet and Prince William Sound, along with changing the name of Ounalaska in the Aleutians: 1) Unalaska 2) Seldovia 3) Homer 4) Sunrise 5) Tyonek 6) Orca

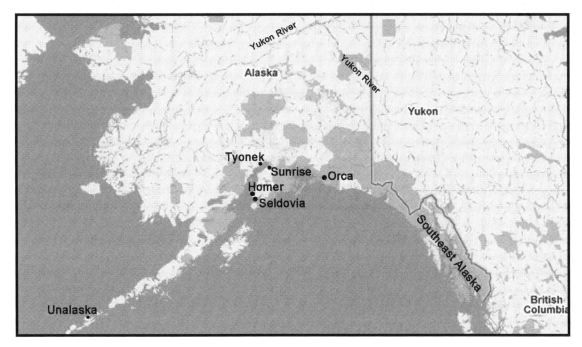

UNIT 4: ROUTES TO RESOURCES

LESSON 13: ALASKA'S PIONEERING POSTMEN

FACTS TO KNOW

Ben S. Downing – Developed the first mail route from Dawson to Nome
Fred Lockley – A mail carrier who started the first mail delivery service in Nome
Ben Taylor – Worked with Fred Lockley to start the first mail delivery service in Nome

COMPREHENSION QUESTIONS

1) Where was the first post office in Alaska under the U.S. government located? When was it established?
Sitka has the honor of being the first post office in the territory under the U.S. government. It was established on July 23, 1867, with John. H. Kincaid (later an Alaska governor) as first postmaster three months before Alaska was formally transferred from Russia to America. (Page 138)

2) What was mail communication like when Alaska was under Russian rule?
The Russians maintained no postal system in Alaska. All communications between Russia and Russian America was carried on via dispatch cases transported by Russian supply ships, and Russian residents dispatched and received both business and personal mail through the Russian commanders of the community – there was no post office system as we know it. (Page 138)

3) News of the Klondike Gold Rush in 1897 brought *Ben S. Downing* north from the Black Hills of South Dakota. He didn't mine for gold, however. Instead he set up the first mail route from *Dawson* to *Nome*.

4) *Nome* was the largest general delivery address in the U.S. postal system during the summer of 1900. In his book, "Alaska's First Free Mail Delivery" in 1900, letter carrier *Fred Lockley* noted that the *postal clerks* had to use five filing boxes just to sort letters for people named Johnson.

5) How did Fred Lockley and Ben Taylor come up with the idea to start the first free mail delivery service to businesses in Nome?
They took leave from their mail carrier duties in Salem, Oregon, to sift for gold in Nome. It was while Lockley and his friend were standing in a more than block-long line at the post office that he conceived the idea of free mail delivery to businesses in Nome. He suggested it to the postal clerk in charge and was hired on the spot. (Page 144)

6) Name three challenges that the early postal carriers faced in Nome.
Mailmen had to deal with frequent relocations in the hustle and bustle of gold-rush Nome. They put in long hours when ships carrying mail arrived in port. Sometimes postmen spent up to 24 hours sorting, routing and even delivering mail. Early postmen had to establish their own routes because there were no roads and very few Native trails. (Pages 138, 147-148)

7) What are some of the ways that the post office attempted to transport the mail around Alaska? What modes of transport worked the best and why?
With the gold rushes came the first attempt to introduce horses to deliver mail, but deep snow proved too much of a handicap. Next, reindeer and dogs were tried. The reindeer proved intractable and impossible to harness break, so it was up to the dogs. In Interior Alaska, the dog team was the first to prove successful in carrying the mail – until the airplane came along. (Page 152)

DISCUSSION QUESTION

(Discuss this question with your teacher or write your answer in essay form below. Use additional paper if necessary.)

How did the people of Nome treat the postmen?

_____
_____
_____
_____
_____
_____
_____
_____

ENRICHMENT ACTIVITY

Imagine that you are a journalist for a newspaper in Nome, and you have been assigned to write a story about the first free mail delivery service in the territory. Write an article about the new service. Share details and quotes from the lesson, such as how the postmen were received by the people of Nome and the process that the mailmen received, sorted and delivered the mail.

LEARN MORE

Read more about Fred Lockley by visiting https://oregonencyclopedia.org/articles/lockley_fred_1871_1958_/#.WMC75zvyvIU

Clum's Post Offices

Word Search Puzzle Key

Find the words listed below

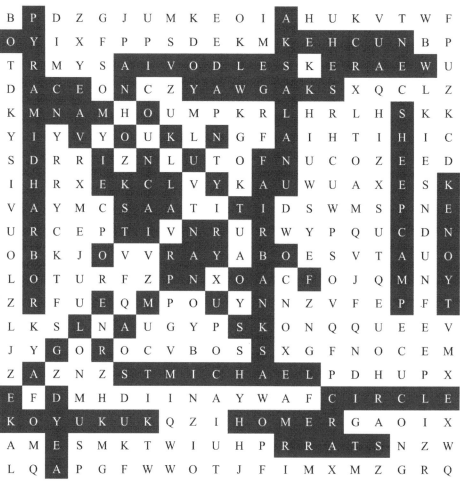

B	P	D	Z	G	J	U	M	K	E	O	I	A	H	U	K	V	T	W	F
O	Y	I	X	F	P	P	S	D	E	K	M	K	E	H	C	U	N	B	P
T	R	M	Y	S	A	I	V	O	D	L	E	S	K	E	R	A	E	W	U
D	A	C	E	O	N	C	Z	Y	A	W	G	A	K	S	X	Q	C	L	Z
K	M	N	A	M	H	O	U	M	P	K	R	L	H	R	L	H	S	K	K
Y	I	Y	V	Y	O	U	K	L	N	G	F	A	I	H	T	I	H	I	C
S	D	R	R	I	Z	N	L	U	T	O	F	N	U	C	O	Z	E	E	D
I	H	R	X	E	K	C	L	V	Y	K	A	U	W	U	A	X	E	S	K
V	A	Y	M	C	S	A	A	T	I	T	I	D	S	W	M	S	P	N	E
U	R	C	E	P	T	I	V	N	R	U	R	W	Y	P	Q	U	C	D	N
O	B	K	J	O	V	V	R	A	Y	A	B	O	E	S	V	T	A	U	O
L	O	T	U	R	F	Z	P	N	X	O	A	C	F	O	J	Q	M	N	Y
Z	R	F	U	E	Q	M	P	O	U	Y	N	N	Z	V	F	E	P	F	T
L	K	S	L	N	A	U	G	Y	P	S	K	O	N	Q	Q	U	E	E	V
J	Y	G	O	R	O	C	V	B	O	S	S	X	G	F	N	O	C	E	M
Z	A	Z	N	Z	S	T	M	I	C	H	A	E	L	P	D	H	U	P	X
E	F	D	M	H	D	I	I	N	A	Y	W	A	F	C	I	R	C	L	E
K	O	Y	U	K	U	K	Q	Z	I	H	O	M	E	R	G	A	O	I	X
A	M	E	S	M	K	T	W	I	U	H	P	R	R	A	T	S	N	Z	W
L	Q	A	P	G	F	W	W	O	T	J	F	I	M	X	M	Z	G	R	Q

SHEEP CAMP	PYRAMID HARBOR	STARR
CANYON	DYEA	SKAGWAY
EAGLE	CIRCLE	FORT YUKON
RAMPART	WEARE	KOYUKUK
NULATO	ANVIK	ST MICHAEL
NOME	UNALASKA	TYONEK
SUNRISE	HOMER	SELDOVIA
NUCHEK	ORCA	FAIRBANKS

UNIT 4: ROUTES TO RESOURCES

LESSON 14: THE TRAPPING LIFE

FACTS TO KNOW

Alaska Commercial Company – Held a monopoly on the fur trade
Trapper – A person who traps wild animals for fur, usually to sell or trade
Ed Ueeck – Alaskan trapper during the 1930s

COMPREHENSION QUESTIONS

1) The Athabascan people came to depend on many items brought north by the white men, including:
Cotton fabric, gunpowder and shot, tea and sugar combs, soap, flour, tobacco, butcher knives and pocket knives. (Page 160)

2) In addition to having a monopoly on the fur trade in Alaska, in what industries did the Alaska Commercial Company participate?
From 1868 through the gold-rush era of the early 1900s, Alaska Commercial Company provided groceries and general merchandise for trappers, explorers and stampeders. The company also served as the bank by extending credit to trappers, miners and fishermen. (Page 161)

3) Established throughout Alaska, village stores became the center of all community activities. They served as the *post office, community hall, courtroom, marriage parlor, funeral home and a safe haven for travelers. (Page 161)*

4) Why did the Alaska Commercial Company change its name to the Northern Commercial Company in 1922? To where did the company headquarters relocate?
A group of employees purchased the company in 1922 and renamed it the Northern Commercial Company. The new owners moved the corporate headquarters to Seattle and the company became a major supplier of heavy equipment and machinery, which contributed to the development of rural Alaska. (Page 162)

5) How did Ed Ueeck become a trapper? How many miles did he travel in an average day to check and reset traps?
He started out helping colonists harvest their crops in the Matanuska Valley. But when he saw the prices paid for furs, he switched professions and turned to trapping. He chose a spot near Lake Leila, on the divide between the Nelchina and Matanuska rivers. He traveled about 14 miles a day to check and reset traps. (Page 165)

6) Describe the trapping life.

After the first hard freeze, they set traps and snares. The winter routine meant checking the trapline, returning to the cabin to skin the animals, stretch the fur and then head out again to check and reset traps. Most families traveled by dog team back to their villages to spend the Christmas holidays, trade their furs and purchase more supplies for the rest of the winter. (Page 163)

DISCUSSION QUESTION

(Discuss this question with your teacher or write your answer in essay form below. Use additional paper if necessary.)

Summarize what you learned about the trapping life from the diary of the "Wildman of Dry Bay."

_____
_____
_____
_____
_____
_____
_____
_____
_____
_____
_____
_____
_____
_____
_____
_____

ENRICHMENT ACTIVITY

Read more about the Athabaskan people by visiting the link below. Write a paragraph about what you learned.
http://www.akhistorycourse.org/alaskas-cultures/alaskas-heritage/chapter-2-3-athabaskans

LEARN MORE

Read more about early trapping and the fur trade by visiting http://www.akhistorycourse.org/americas-territory/alaskas-heritage/chapter-4-14-trading-and-trapping

Natives Trade Furs for Western Goods
Word Scramble Key
Unscramble the words below

1.	onctot rcifab	cotton fabric	A light-weight material from which clothes are made.
2.	prugdwoen	gunpowder	An explosive consisting of a powdered mixture of saltpeter, sulfur and charcoal.
3.	bsnealtk	blankets	Large pieces of woolen or similar material used to cover beds or other coverings for warmth.
4.	augrs	sugar	A sweet crystalline substance obtained from various plants.
5.	bsmoc	combs	Strips of plastic, metal or wood with rows of narrow teeth, used for untangling or arranging the hair.
6.	poas	soap	A substance used with water for washing and cleaning.
7.	rlofu	flour	A powder obtained by grinding grain, typically wheat, and used to make bread, cakes and pastry.
8.	tbaococ	tobacco	Nicotine-rich leaves of an American plant, which are cured by a process of drying and fermentation for smoking or chewing.
9.	vnesik	knives	Sharp blades attached to handles that are used for cutting or as a weapon.
10.	stletke	kettles	Vessels, usually made of metal and with a handle, used for boiling liquids or cooking foods.

UNIT 4: ROUTES TO RESOURCES

LESSON 15: DALTON TURNS TIMBER INTO GOLD

FACTS TO KNOW

Jack Dalton – He established a toll road and built a sawmill in Southeast Alaska
Tlingit Indians – Indigenous people of Southeast Alaska
Sawmill – A facility where logs are cut into timber

COMPREHENSION QUESTIONS

1) Jack Dalton established a _toll road_ from Pyramid Harbor on the Lynn Canal to the _Yukon_ River, on which around 2,000 _cattle_ had traveled and made a welcome addition to many miner's food supply during the _Klondike_ Gold Rush. His trail would later become part of the _Haines Highway_.

2) How did the Tlingit Indians utilize timber? How did they profit from timber when non-Native settlers came to the territory?
They burned wood for heat, made dugouts from cottonwood trees, carved household and ritual items, and stripped bark from cedar trees for weavers of Chilkat blankets. When non-Natives began settling the area, bringing a cash economy with them, the Natives supplied the new settlers with firewood. Soon that became the most common service provided by the Natives for the newcomers. (Page 173)

3) How did Jack Dalton profit from timber in 1899?
Dalton built a sawmill in 1899 that produced 5,000 board feet of lumber a day. The sawmill also made lumber needed for large flumes for the goldmining effort. (Pages 172-173)

4) Where did the lumber come from for major building projects in Alaska, such as Fort Seward in Haines?
The majority of the lumber for major projects was sent via steamship from Seattle or Olympia, Washington, or from Portland, Oregon. Quite a bit of lumber from outside of Alaska was used to build Haines' Fort Seward and many local canneries, although some of the early canneries had small, private mills to use in making fish traps and other small construction projects. (Pages 173-175)

DISCUSSION QUESTION

(Discuss this question with your teacher or write your answer in essay form below. Use additional paper if necessary.)

The Tlingit people and Jack Dalton understood that timber was an important resource that many people needed. What are some things that we use timber for today?

_____

_____

_____

_____

_____

_____

_____

_____

_____

_____

_____

_____

_____

_____

_____

_____

ENRICHMENT ACTIVITY

Watch this five-minute video to see an aerial view of a modern-day sawmill in Washington by visiting https://www.youtube.com/watch?v=NvbgwdTGoyo&t=35s

LEARN MORE

Read more about the lumber industry in Alaska by visiting http://www.akhistorycourse. org/americas-territory/alaskas-heritage/chapter-4-17-farming-herding-and-lumbering

UNIT 4: ROUTES TO RESOURCES

LESSON 16: ROUTES TO GOLD, COPPER AND COAL

FACTS TO KNOW

E.J. Glave – English explorer and traveling companion of Jack Dalton

Matanuska River – 75-mile-long river in Southcentral Alaska

COMPREHENSION QUESTIONS

1) How did E.J. Glave describe Jack Dalton?
"Dalton," Glave wrote later, "is a most desirable partner – has excellent judgment, cool and deliberate in times of danger and possessed of great tact in dealing with the Indians ... as a camp cook, I've never seen his equal." (Page 177)

2) Describe the disagreement between Jack Dalton and the railway company.
Dalton had filed on three mineral claims straddling the 1906 railroad survey that led to the railroad's proposed dock. When company men began laying rails to the dock, Dalton was there with his rifle. Heading for the company's office, he informed the man in charge that the minute any man crossed his property, he would come looking for the foreman and wouldn't stop until he had found him. (Page 180)

3) How was the disagreement in the question above resolved?
The argument ended up in court, which found for the railroad. It decided the land was more valuable as a railroad right-of-way than as mineral land, and Dalton had to remove his trestle that joined the railroad property. It was one battle Dalton didn't win. (Page 181)

4) What task did federal Bureau of Mines director A.M. Holmes give Jack Dalton in 1913?
He gave Dalton the task of figuring out a way to get the coal from the Matanuska Valley to tidewater – at a cost the agency could afford. Coal was being shipped from as far away as Cardiff, Wales, to the U.S. Navy's coal station at Sitka. Some thought that the coal deposits at Chickaloon in the Matanuska Valley might meet the Navy's requirements. (Pages 180-181)

5) What was Jack Dalton's solution to this problem?
Dalton concluded that the Matanuska River, when frozen, could be used part of the way and that horses could convey the coal. As soon as the ice was thick enough, freight began to move. Fifty-four horses pulled five bobsleds, which carried from three to seven tons of coal. By January 1914, 700 tons had been carried as far as Eska Crossing. By Feb. 1, the entire lot had left Chickaloon. (Pages 180-181)

DISCUSSION QUESTION

(Discuss this question with your teacher or write your answer in essay form below. Use additional paper if necessary.)

Jack Dalton was a man that solved the problems that he saw around him. Name another person in history that became famous by solving a problem. Discuss the problem and how this person solved it.

_____
_____
_____
_____
_____
_____
_____
_____
_____
_____
_____
_____
_____
_____
_____
_____
_____
_____

ENRICHMENT ACTIVITY

Read more about Jack Dalton and others who established road transportation in early Alaska by visiting the link below. Take notes and share what you learned orally with the class.

http://www.akhistorycourse.org/americas-territory/alaskas-heritage/chapter-4-10-road-transportation

TIME TO REVIEW

Review Chapters 12-16 of your book before moving on the Unit Review. See how many questions you can answer without looking at your book.

Routes to Resources

Crossword Puzzle

Read Across and Down clues and fill in blank boxes that match numbers on the clues

Across

3 This man's ability to deal with Alaska Natives proved invaluable
4 Small enclosure where trappers kept their food
6 Address used when sending mail if one does not know the exact address of an individual
9 Another name for a postman
13 Business that Jack Dalton built in 1899 that produced 5,000 board feet of lumber a day
16 Jack Dalton definitely was one of these
17 Place where Dalton established his headquarters for coal transportation project
18 Route that trappers followed to trap furbearers
19 These animals were too hard to harness break for mail deliveries
20 Natives sold these foot coverings to stampeders
22 The one battle Dalton did not win involved this mode of transportation
24 Town that was the largest general delivery address in the United States in 1900
28 In the 1920s, these spelled the end to dog teams delivering mail in Alaska
29 These people sold 75,000 pelts to traders in 1880
31 A sawmill, which was the first business built, owned and operated by Natives in Alaska, was at this location
32 This was piled 10-20 feet high along Nome's waterfront in 1900
36 Type of boats that Alaska Natives made from timber in Southeast Alaska
38 Dalton went to this city to get men, supplies and horses for the Matanuska Valley coal transportation project
39 What postmen deliver
40 What one puts on mail to show the postage has been paid to send it

Down

1 Mailman Ben Downing would get angry if one of these was stolen from a shelter
2 This adventurer, who became a trader, was convinced that gold extended from the Yukon into Alaska
3 How Ben Downing delivered mail
5 Deep snow proved too much for these animals to carry the mail
7 Method Russians used to send mail
8 Battleship that tested the Matanuska Valley coal
10 When trapping season ended
11 Dalton figured out how to get this valuable resource from the Matanuska Valley down to tidewater
12 This activity drove economic activity following America's purchase of Alaska
14 Type of tool used to catch furbearing animals
15 Unusual place that many miners gave in order to get their mail delivered
21 Quality coal deposits from this area met U.S. Navy requirements
23 Boats that carried freight from steamships to the beach of Nome
25 Preferring to use spruce for these, Alaska Natives took these apart and made tools
26 These were built about 25 miles apart on a mail route

Routes to Resources
Crossword Puzzle Key

Down (Continued)

27 Mail carrier from Oregon who traveled to Alaska when gold was discovered at Nome
30 About 2,000 of this type of animal crossed Jack Dalton's toll road during the Klondike Gold Rush era
33 Jack Dalton and this man decided to solve the "defective transportation" problem in Alaska
34 What mail is carried in for delivery
35 Editor of the *Tombstone Epitaph* who became the post office inspector for Alaska in 1898
37 Man who started out harvesting crops and then became a trapper between Nelchina and Matanuska rivers

Courtesy Alaska State Library

Above: Dalton Transportation Company did a good business hauling supplies across the White Pass Trail during the Klondike Gold Rush. Sometimes Jack Dalton used oxen to pull loaded sleds, as seen in this photograph taken on April 2, 1899.

Below: U.S. President Warren G. Harding, seen here seated on a bear skin on the steps of the government coal mine in Chickaloon, visited Alaska to help celebrate the completion of the Alaska Railroad in 1923. The coal mine had shut down the year before his visit.

Courtesy Alaska State Library

UNIT 4: ROUTES TO RESOURCES

REVIEW LESSONS 12-16

Write down what you remember about:

John Clum – _Editor of the Tombstone Epitaph and the first appointed post office inspector_

Ben S. Downing – _Developed the first mail route from Dawson to Nome_

Fred Lockley – _A mail carrier who started the first mail delivery service in Nome_

Ben Taylor – _Worked with Fred Lockley to start the first mail delivery service in Nome_

Alaska Commercial Company – _Held a monopoly on the fur trade_

Trapper – _A person who traps wild animals for fur, usually to sell or trade_

Ed Ueeck – _Alaskan trapper during the 1930s_

Jack Dalton – _He established a toll road and built a sawmill in Southeast Alaska_

Tlingit Indians – _Indigenous people of Southeast Alaska_

Sawmill – _A facility where logs are cut into timber_

E.J. Glave – _English explorer and traveling companion of Jack Dalton_

Matanuska River – _75-mile-long river in Southcentral Alaska_

Fill in the blanks:

1) The colorful _editor_ of the famous _Tombstone Epitaph_ made his mark on Alaska in the late _1890s_. _John Clum_ also became the first mayor of _Tombstone,_ and it was during this era that the legendary gunfight at the OK Corral was fought.

2) But it was another one of _Clum's_ ventures that brought him to Alaska and gave him the opportunity to leave his mark on the new land. In March 1898, he was appointed _post office inspector_ for the territory.

3) As _post office inspector_, _John Clum_ set up post offices in Southeast Alaska, along the _Yukon River_ and then down to the _Aleutian Chain_, where he changed the name of the post office at Ounalaska to _Unalaska_.

4) _Ben S. Downing_ came north from the Black Hills of South Dakota following the discovery of _gold_ in the Klondike. He took the job of creating the first mail route from _Dawson_ to _Nome_.

5) It was while _Fred Lockely_ and his friend, _Ben Taylor_, were standing in a more than block-long line at the post office that he conceived the idea of _free mail delivery_ to businesses in _Nome_. _John Clum_, the post office inspector, wrote up the letter authorizing the plan and sent _Lockley_ and _Taylor_ on their way.

6) Sometimes postmen spent up to _24_ hours _sorting, routing_ and _delivering_ the massive amount of mail when several _ships_ unloaded simultaneously. But the mail didn't just arrive by _ships_. It also came by _dog team_ from places like Dawson.

7) Postal employees' normal schedules involved from _10 to 12_ hours per day. The dedicated mailmen also had to contend with patrons' frequent _relocations_ in the hustle and bustle of gold-rush Nome.

8) With the gold rushes came the first attempt to introduce _horses_ as beasts of burden in the new land of ice and snow, but _deep snow_ proved too much of a handicap. Next, _reindeer_ and _dogs_ were tried. The _reindeer_ proved intractable and impossible to harness break, so it was up to the _dogs_. In Interior Alaska, the _dog team_ was the first mode of transportation to prove successful in carrying the mail – until the _airplane_ came along.

9) Trapping worked out well for many families because they could live their _subsistence lifestyles_ in the summer months. After the first hard freeze, they set _traps and snares._ The winter routine meant checking the _trapline_, returning to the cabin to _skin_ the animals, _stretch_ the fur and then head out again to _check and reset_ traps. Most families traveled by _dog team_ back to their villages to spend the Christmas holidays, _trade_ their furs and purchase more _supplies_ for the rest of the winter.

10) After establishing the first _toll road_ in the territory, _Jack Dalton_ had an area around the Porcupine gold field surveyed – 36 miles from Haines up the Chilkat Valley – he realized that more gold lay in the _forested area_ surrounding the town site. He built a _sawmill_ in 1899 that produced 5,000 _board feet of lumber_ a day.

11) Jack Dalton's traveling partner, _E.J. Glave_, wrote this about him:
"Dalton is a most desirable partner – has _excellent judgment_, cool and deliberate in times of danger and possessed _of great tact_ in dealing with the _Indians_… as a camp cook, I've never seen his equal."

12) _Gold, copper_ then _coal_ challenged Dalton's trailblazing talents. Some thought that the _coal_ deposits at Chickaloon in the _Matanuska_ Valley might meet the U.S. Navy's requirements.

13) Along with federal _Bureau of Mines_ director A.M. Holmes, Dalton went to look the mine over in the year _1913_. Dalton received the task _of figuring out a way to get the coal from the mine to tidewater_ – at a cost the agency could afford.

14) Dalton successfully transported _coal_ from the _Matanuska Valley_ to tidewater to be used by the U.S. Navy. After the ice went out of the Inlet, the coal was placed aboard the battleship _USS Maryland_ for testing. But before anything could be done about providing a regular supply of _coal_, the Navy converted to _oil_.

UNIT 4: ROUTES TO RESOURCES

UNIT TEST

Choose *two* of the following questions to answer in paragraph form. Use as much detail as possible to completely answer the question.

1) Who was John Clum? Name two of his ventures. What venture brought him to Alaska? Was his job in Alaska easy or hard? Explain your answer.

2) Describe how the first free postal delivery service in Nome started. Who started it? How did he come up with the idea? What need did he see in Nome?

3) What is a trapper? Why was trapping an important business in early Alaska? Briefly describe what a year for a trapping family was like in early Alaska.

4) Describe Jack Dalton. Name two ventures for which Jack Dalton was famous. Explain how he got involved in each venture.

_____

_____

_____

_____

_____

_____

_____

_____

_____

_____

_____

_____

_____

_____

_____

_____

_____

_____

TEACHER NOTES ABOUT THIS UNIT

UNIT 5: PRINCE WILLIAM SOUND

LESSON 17: GLACIER TRAIL BIRTHS VALDEZ

FACTS TO KNOW

Valdez Glacier Trail – A trail along the Valdez Glacier that many stampeders traveled to find gold along the Copper River

Copper Center – A settlement at the confluence of the Klutina and Copper rivers

Scurvy – A disease resulting from lack of vitamin C; often from lack of fruits and vegetables in one's diet

Port Valdez – Gold seekers formed a tent city here in 1898

COMPREHENSION QUESTIONS

1) According to the authors of *Valdez Gold Rush Trails of 1898-99*, what was one of the greatest hoaxes in Alaska's history? Why did they call it a hoax?
The Valdez Glacier Trail was promoted as the "best trail" to get to the Copper River and find even more gold than the Klondike. When prospectors got to the trail, they found a glacier that was twice as big as advertised. (Page 184)

2) What kind of conditions did prospectors find while traveling the Valdez Glacier Trail?
The adventurers encountered all sorts of conditions, including snow slides, snow blindness, glacial crevasses and extreme physical challenges as they pulled their supply-laden sleds. The rugged pioneers made as many as 20 trips back and forth over the steepest legs of the journey in order to transport the necessary year's worth of supplies. (Page 186)

3) Not all the thousands of prospectors that crossed the glacial trail were men. Name one of the women who made it across the trail. What did she do after she crossed the trail?
(Students may give one of the following answers:)
a) A Mrs. Dowling became a living legend when she nursed a U.S. Army man stricken with typhoid back to health at Klutina Lake. She also inspired stampeders who were ready to quit and go home.
b) Mrs. Anne Barrett, famous for her fresh lingonberry pies, opened an eatery at Klutina Lake and also became a mine owner at Slate Creek. She later opened a restaurant in Valdez.
c) Lillian Moore, who was an excellent horsewoman, hired on with U.S. Army Lt. W.R. Abercrombie and guided horses over the Valdez Glacier. She and her husband later operated a transport company and took horse-drawn sleds over what became the Richardson Trail. (Pages 186-187)

4) Why was there a scurvy epidemic in Copper City during the winter of 1898-1899?
Many developed scurvy because they subsisted primarily on bacon and beans. Scurvy reached epidemic proportions in Copper Center that winter, necessitating heroic rescues, emergency deliveries of food from Valdez and specialized medical care. (Page 189)

5) When was Port Valdez established? To whom did the area belong before the European explorers arrived?
Port Valdez was named in 1790 by Don Salvador Fidalgo for the celebrated Spanish Admiral Antonio Valdes y Basan who was head of the Spanish Marines and Minister of the Indies at the time. Historically, the territory south of Valdez belongs to the Chugach Eskimo, a maritime hunting people, and to the north the land is of the Ahtna, an Athabascan people of the Copper River Basin. A tent city sprang up at the head of the bay, and as some stampeders stayed on shore to set up shops and businesses, Valdez grew into a supply center. (Pages 189-190)

DISCUSSION QUESTION

(Discuss this question with your teacher or write your answer in essay form below. Use additional paper if necessary.)

Think about all the gold rush cities that we have studied in this book so far (and in Volume 1, if you read it). Do you see any similarities in the impact the gold rush had on these cities? What seemed to happen to the cities when the gold rush ended in those locations?

_____
_____
_____
_____
_____
_____
_____
_____
_____
_____
_____
_____
_____
_____
_____
_____
_____

ENRICHMENT ACTIVITY

Imagine that you are a medical professional in Alaska during the gold rush period. You are tired of treating so many scurvy patients, so you decide to create a flyer to educate stampeders about what scurvy is and how to prevent it. Create your flyer using information from the lesson and any additional resources.

You can read more about symptoms of scurvy, what it is and how to prevent it by visiting: http://www.bbc.co.uk/history/british/empire_seapower/captaincook_scurvy_01.shtml

LEARN MORE

Read more about early Alaska railroads in Valdez, Cordova and other areas by visiting http://www.akhistorycourse.org/americas-territory/alaskas-heritage/chapter-4-11-railroad-transportation

UNIT 5: PRINCE WILLIAM SOUND

LESSON 18: CORDOVA – A TOWN BORN OF STRIFE

FACTS TO KNOW

Cordova – A small town located near the Copper River

Michael J. Heney – Irish railroad contractor who thought that Cordova would be a good spot for a railroad

Guggenheim-Morgan Syndicate – Companies that partnered and attempted to monopolize the coal resources in Alaska

COMPREHENSION QUESTIONS

1) Why was it important to have a railroad through Cordova? What did Michael Heney discover when he surveyed the railway route?

A railroad was needed to carry coal from the Wrangell mountains past the two large glaciers. There was no other form of transportation to carry the coal, oil and copper. (Page 195)

2) What obstacles were in the way of building the railroad over Michael Heney's route?

Before Heney could build the railroad over this route, he had to persuade the Guggenheim-Morgan Syndicate that the route was feasible. The syndicate tried a route from Katalla, 40 miles east of Cordova. But other railroads were being built from there, also, and rival railroad gangs often clashed. (Page 197)

3) What was early Cordova like?

It was a typical construction town in 1908, where men worked and played hard. It had the enthusiasm and energy of youth. Optimism ran high, and Cordova businessmen were sure the region, with its resources of copper, coal and oil, had a bright future. (Page 198)

4) What happened in 1907 when the Valdez railroad men attempted to break down the Guggenheim-Morgan Syndicate's rock barricade at Keystone Canyon?

Armed with tools, Valdez railroad men marched toward the syndicate's obstruction on Sept. 25, 1907, and were met with gunfire backed by badges. Local syndicate officials had convinced the U.S. marshal in Fairbanks to issue temporary deputy marshal commissions to syndicate employees, including a man named Edward C. Hasey. Sheltered behind the barricade, Hasey shot three marchers, killing one. The syndicate paid off witnesses in order to get Hasey off. (Page 201)

5) How did the incident at Keystone Canyon eventually lead to the end of the syndicate's ability to monopolize coal resources in Alaska?

The attorney general decided to reopen the investigation into the Keystone Canyon trials and other questionable activities of the syndicate in Alaska after Judge Wickersham found evidence that the syndicate had paid off witnesses and jurors. Federal officials determined that the claims had been taken out with intent to consolidate and create a monopoly in the interests of the Guggenheim-Morgan Syndicate. That discovery brought about the prosecution of several syndicate officials. (Pages 201-202)

6) Why did 300 residents of Cordova march to the Alaska Steamship Company dock in 1911? Did the marchers get the result that they wanted?
Many Alaskans' dreams of riches from coal and oil dried up when Gifford Pinchot , U.S. Forest Service director, ordered the withdrawal of those coalfield holdings to protect them from the Guggenheim Syndicate. Communities had to start importing coal from Canada, and many Alaskans resented being forced to purchase high-dollar coal from foreigners when Alaska had an abundance of coal. (Page 203)

DISCUSSION

(Discuss this question with your teacher or write your answer in essay form below. Use additional paper if necessary.)

Compare what you know about the Cordova Coal Party and the Boston Tea Party. What are some similarities? What are some differences?

_____
_____
_____
_____
_____
_____
_____
_____
_____
_____
_____
_____
_____
_____
_____
_____
_____
_____

LEARN MORE

Read more about the fight for railroads by visiting http://www.akhistorycourse.org/southcentral-alaska/1900-1915-fight-for-a-railroad

MAP ACTIVITY

Find these on the map below: 1) Port Valdez 2) Cordova 3) Copper River 4) Keystone Canyon

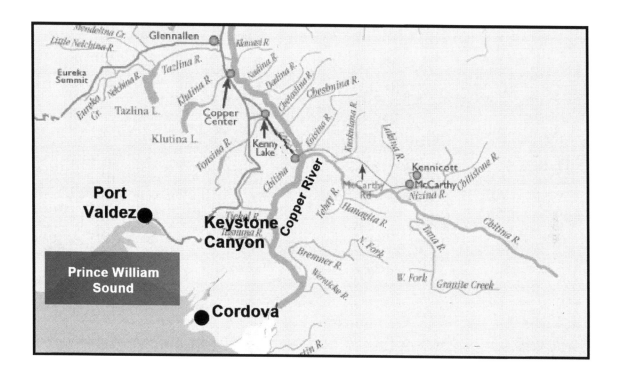

UNIT 5: PRINCE WILLIAM SOUND

LESSON 19: SEWARD'S RESURRECTIONS

FACTS TO KNOW

Alexander Baranof – Russian explorer who named (Voskresenskaya Gavan) Resurrection Bay in 1792

Seward – Small town named after Secretary of State William H. Seward

John Ballaine – Founder of the town of Seward

COMPREHENSION QUESTIONS

1) What led Alexander Baranof to Resurrection Bay? Why did he name it Resurrection Bay?

Russian explorer Alexander Baranof named the sheltered bay, finding it a welcome refuge from Pacific storms. Since it was the Easter season when he first saw it, he named it "Voskresenskaya Gavan," meaning "Resurrection (Sunday) Harbor." (Page 210)

2) Why did John Ballaine want to name the town of Seward after Secretary of State William H. Seward?

The founder was convinced the new city would one day be the metropolis of a great territory and should fittingly bear the name of the man who foresaw the primacy of the Pacific Ocean in the world's future. In March 1903, he bestowed upon the new town the name of Seward. (Pages 213-214)

3) What issue did the postal inspector have with naming the town Seward? How did John Ballaine resolve this matter?

The postal inspector of the district embracing Alaska filed a protest against calling the embryo city on Resurrection Bay Seward, arguing that there were already several Sewards in the territory. Ballaine wrote a letter to President Theodore Roosevelt, who agreed that the town should be named after Secretary of State Seward. Ballaine had won his point and Seward was officially recognized and founded on Aug. 28, 1903. (Pages 214-215)

4) How did Seward go from a booming construction town in 1903 to a town waiting for resurrection within a decade?

The boom collapsed when the "powers that be" in Washington decided to conserve Alaska coal, and all coal lands in Alaska were withdrawn from entry. The Alaska Central Railroad went bankrupt in 1908, but re-emerged as the Alaska Northern in 1910. At no time was the railroad even able to earn out-of-pocket expenses. Its "tracks, bridges and docks were not adequately maintained, and by 1915 it was hardly in operating condition...." The boomers left. (Page 216)

5) What happened in 1914 to resurrect the town?

The U.S. government chose Seward as the saltwater terminus for its proposed government railroad. Houses, which the owners would have practically given away, were selling at boom prices by the afternoon of the announcement, and choice lots were swallowed up by speculators. New stores opened and stores already there worked feverishly to expand and enlarge. Building went on around the clock. Thousands of men came to Seward to work on the railroad. (Page 217)

DISCUSSION QUESTION

(Discuss this question with your teacher or write your answer in essay form below. Use additional paper if necessary.)

Do you know the story behind the name of your hometown? Was it named after a special person? If you don't know, do a little research at your local library or online.

_____

_____

_____

_____

_____

_____

_____

_____

_____

_____

_____

_____

_____

_____

_____

_____

LEARN MORE

Look for this book at your local library:
The Copper Spike, Lone E. Janson. Anchorage: Alaska Northwest Publishing Company, 1975.

TIME TO REVIEW

Review Chapters 17-19 of your book before moving on the Unit Review. See how many questions you can answer without looking at your book.

Prince William Sound Develops
Word Scramble Puzzle Key
Unscramble the words below

1.	dlevaz	valdez	A glacier birthed this town as it grew into a supply center in late 1890s
2.	hrdsnrcaio	richardson	The Keystone Canyon Trail eventually became this highway
3.	ghcchua	chugach	Historically the territory south of Valdez belongs to these people
4.	ahtna	ahtna	Historically the territory north of Valdez belongs to these people
5.	lcsumi	liscum	Fort first located three miles from the head of Valdez Bay
6.	oradasrli	railroads	Companies building these caused considerable turmoil in Prince William Sound in the early 1900s
7.	ydolrnse	reynolds	The man who convinced investors to support the Alaska Home Railroad, which left people with no jobs and little money when it flopped
8.	peopcr	copper	A mountain of this was found in the Wrangell Mountains in the early 1900s
9.	voocard	cordova	Town born when engineers chose its location to be the terminus of a railroad to carry precious ore from the Kennecott mines
10.	yehen	heney	Irish contractor who surveyed a railroad route through glaciers

Prince William Sound Develops
Word Scramble Puzzle Key
Continued

11. farbaon	baranof	Man who named Resurrection Bay
12. lonilmi olardl	million dollar	Name of bridge at the glaciers along the route of the Copper River and Northwestern Railway
13. latalka	katalla	Town in the heart of oil and coalfields 40 miles east of Cordova
14. cdnetaysi	syndicate	The Guggenheim/Morgan companies, which owned copper and coal mines near Cordova, are one of these
15. thopnci	pinchot	First director of the U.S. Forest Service who ordered the withdrawal of vast coalfield
16. adrswe	seward	This town on Resurrection Bay started out in 1902 from a plan to build a railroad
17. lenaialb	ballaine	Man who chose the name for Seward
18. ausitvk	vituska	The first name of the town that became Seward
19. seeoltvor	roosevelt	U.S. President who gave approval to the name Seward
20. asalak cnrtale	alaska central	Railroad in Seward that went bankrupt in 1908

UNIT 5: PRINCE WILLIAM SOUND

REVIEW LESSONS 17-19

Write down what you remember about:

Valdez Glacier Trail – _A trail along the Valdez Glacier that many stampeders traveled to find gold along the Copper River_

Copper Center – _A settlement at the confluence of the Klutina and Copper rivers_

Scurvy – _A disease resulting from lack of vitamin C; often from lack of fruits and vegetables in one's diet_

Port Valdez – _Gold seekers formed a tent city here in 1898_

Cordova – _A small town located near the Copper River_

Michael J. Heney – _Irish railroad contractor who thought that Cordova would be a good spot for a railroad_

Guggenheim-Morgan Syndicate – _Companies that partnered and attempted to monopolize the coal resources in Alaska_

Alexander Baranof – _Russian explorer who named (Voskresenskaya Gavan) Resurrection Bay in 1792_

Seward – _Small town named after Secretary of State William H. Seward_

John Ballaine – _Founder of the town of Seward_

Fill in the blanks:

1) "Gold in Alaska!" "_Valdez Glacier_ – Best Trail!" rang the headlines in _1897-1898_. Promoters of this route claimed that prospectors would find more gold in the _American_ soil along the _Copper_ River than they would in the Canadian _Klondike_. And that was one of the greatest _hoaxes_ in Alaska's history, according to Jim and Nancy Lethcoe in their book, _Valdez Gold Rush Trails of 1898-99._

2) Some stampeders who made it over the glacier stayed in Port _Valdez,_ named in 1790 by Don Salvador Fidalgo. Salvador also named _Cordova_, Port _Gravina_ and other spots while on his voyage to Alaska to investigate the extent of Russian involvement and to reestablish _Spanish_ claim to the area.

3) The shooting of a Valdez railroad worker on a barricaded track in _Keystone_ Canyon on September 25, _1907_, resulted in payoffs, perjury and manipulation by the _Guggenheim-Morgan_ Syndicate and ended the syndicate's attempt to control _coal_ resources in Alaska.

4) Many Alaskans' dreams of riches from _coal_ and _oil_ dried up when Gifford Pinchot , U.S. Forest Service director, ordered the withdrawal of those coalfield holdings to protect them from the _Guggenheim-Morgan Syndicate_. Communities had to start importing _coal_ from _Canada_, and many Alaskans resented being forced to purchase high-dollar _coal_ from foreigners when Alaska had an abundance of the resource.

5) Shovels in hand, 300 _Cordovans_ marched down to the Alaska Steamship Company dock in 1911. They formed the _Cordova Coal Party_, and shouted "Give us Alaska coal," as several tons of _Canadian coal_ were dumped into the bay.

6) Russian explorer _Alexander Baranof_ named _Resurrection_ Bay in 1792.

7) Founder _John Ballaine_ was convinced the city of _Seward_ would one day be the metropolis of a great territory and should fittingly bear the name of the man who foresaw the primacy of the Pacific Ocean in the world's future, Secretary of State _William H. Seward._

8) _Seward_ became a roaring construction town, but the boom collapsed when the "powers that be" in Washington decided to conserve Alaska _coal_. The _Alaska Central Railroad_ went bankrupt in 1908, but re-emerged as the _Alaska Northern_ in 1910.

9) At no time was the railroad even able to earn _out-of-pocket expenses_. Its tracks, bridges and docks were not adequately maintained, and by _1915_ it was hardly in operating condition. _Seward_ soon became a town waiting for a _resurrection_.

10) The U.S. government had chosen _Seward_ as the saltwater terminus for its proposed _government railroad_. The boom was on again. From the states arrived boatloads of men seeking work on _the new railroad._

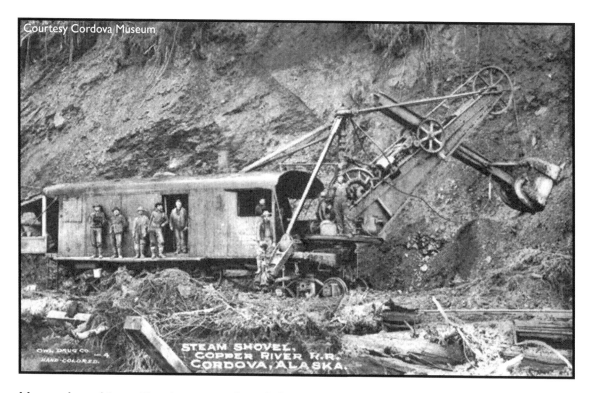

STEAM SHOVEL.
COPPER RIVER R.R.
CORDOVA, ALASKA.

Men and machines, like the steam shovel above, worked hard to get copper and coal out of the mountains in Alaska. They also worked tirelessly to build the community of Cordova, seen below. This photo shows First Avenue in 1909.

FIRST AVE CORDOVA, ALASKA.

UNIT 5: PRINCE WILLIAM SOUND

UNIT TEST

Choose *two* of the following questions to answer in paragraph form. Use as much detail as possible to completely answer the question.

1) Why was the promotion of the Valdez Glacier Trail called one of the biggest hoaxes in Alaska's history? What kind of conditions did prospectors find when they got there? What city was formed as a result of the thousands of stampeders that came to cross the glacier?

2) How did the Guggenheim-Morgan Syndicate attempt to monopolize coal resources in Alaska? What happened at Keystone Canyon in 1907? How did this eventually result in ruining Guggenheim-Morgan Syndicate's plan to monopolize coal in Alaska?

3) Explain why railroad transportation was important in Alaska during the early 1900s What were some of the obstacles that the railroad companies had to face in order to build the railroads?

4) Describe the town of Seward. Who founded it? Who was the town named after and why? Why did the town need a resurrection in 1914? What happened to cause a second boom in 1914?

TEACHER NOTES ABOUT THIS UNIT

UNIT 6: WILDERNESS TRAILS

LESSON 20: SLED DOGS LEAD THE WAY
LESSON 21: BLAZING THE IDITAROD TRAIL

Note: Read both chapters 20 and 21 before completing this lesson.

FACTS TO KNOW

Sled dog team – A group of dogs trained to pull a sled for travel
Lead dog – The dog that leads the sled dog team
Iditarod Trail – The approximately 1,000-mile route from Seward to Nome
Walter Goodwin – Hired by the Alaska Road Commission to scout a trail from Seward to Nome

COMPREHENSION QUESTIONS

1) In what ways did Native Alaskans utilize sled dogs during the 1700-1800s?
Alaska Natives used dogs to haul sleds loaded with fish, game, wood and other items. The Natives ran ahead of the dogs as they guided them on the yearly trips between villages and fish and hunting camps. (Page 220)

2) How did the Russian Explorers improve upon the sled dog system?
Russians improved the sled dog system by adding handlebars to sleds and harnessing dog teams in single file or in pairs. They also trained the dogs to follow commands given by sled drivers and introduced the "lead dog" or leader. (Page 220)

3) Why were sled dogs in even greater demand during the late 1890s and early 1900s?
Extensive use of dogs for long-distance transportation developed as gold discoveries were made in the late 1890s and early 1900s. Stampeders quickly learned that dog teams were worth their weight in gold. Thousands of dogs were imported from the contiguous states to help prospectors and adventurers reach the gold fields. (Pages 220-221)

4) How did Iditarod become the largest town in Alaska for a brief period in the early 1900s?
John Beaton and William Dikeman discovered gold along the Haiditarod River, a tributary of the Innoko, in the area that soon would become the Iditarod Mining District. The men told a steamboat crew about their find as they traveled to Takotna to record their claims. Word spread, and within a year the last full-scale gold rush in American history boomed in an incredibly remote section of Alaska. (Pages 228-229)

5) What trail did Walter Goodwin establish in 1911? Why was this trail important?
New strikes along the Innoko River called for a more direct route from Seward to Nome through the Cook Inlet country. Whereas Nome and the Cook Inlet areas were easily accessible by ocean steamers, Interior gold strikes – the Iditarod, Innoko and Ruby districts – were isolated. Goodwin was ordered by Maj. Wilds P. Richardson to scout out the trail from Seward to Nome, later called the Iditarod Trail. (Pages 228-299)

6) Who was Jujiro Wada? What did the city of Seward hire him to do?
Jujiro Wada, after mushing from Fairbanks to Dawson to help spread word of the gold discovery in Alaska's Interior, blazed a trail to the Innoko mining area in 1909. He became one of Alaska's best non-Native mushers. And during the goldrush era, when most Asians were common laborers, Wada's mushing exploits filled the northern press. (Page 229)

DISCUSSION QUESTION

(Discuss this question with your teacher or write your answer in essay form below. Use additional paper if necessary.)

What do you think it was like for early Russian settlers in Alaska to begin traveling by sled dog teams?

_____
_____
_____
_____
_____
_____
_____
_____
_____
_____
_____

ENRICHMENT ACTIVITY

Learn more about sled dogs by watching this short YouTube video:
https://www.youtube.com/watch?v=6nVfFNbxX7s

LEARN MORE

Look for this book at your local library:
Everything I Know About Training and Racing Sled Dogs, George Attla. Rome, New York: Arner Publications, 1974.

UNIT 6: WILDERNESS TRAILS

LESSON 22: IDITAROD TRAIL PHOTO ESSAY

Fill in the blanks:

1) _Sled dogs_ have a long and illustrious past in the Great North. Natives bred _dogs,_ which became part of Alaskan families' everyday lives, for survival in the harsh climate. Two breeds were most common: _Alaska malamutes and Siberian huskies_.

2) The large _malamute dogs_ mostly were used for pulling heavy loads of _fish, game and supplies_ between camps and villages. _Siberian huskies_ were exported to Alaska during the gold-rush era and used for transportation of _people and goods_.

3) The town of _Iditarod_ grew out of the wilderness after prospectors _John Beaton_ and _William Dikeman_ discovered gold along the _Haiditarod_ River, a tributary of the Innoko, in December 1908.

4) A _sled dog_ team pulled into _Seward_ on Dec. 23, 1910, carrying one-half ton of gold dust, valued at $210,000, from the _Iditarod_ gold fields. Consigned to Brown and Hawkins, it was the largest gold dust shipment ever carried by _dog_ team in Alaska.

5) The blazing of the _Iditarod_ Trail opened a new route to transport the precious gold from _Nome_ to _Seward_. _Tent roadhouses_ popped up along the _Iditarod_ Trail before more substantial structures were built.

ENRICHMENT ACTIVITY

Choose one or two pictures from the lesson, and write your own paragraph about each picture. Make up your own story about what is going on in the picture.

LEARN MORE

Look for this article at your local library:
"Is Alaska Mining an Endangered Industry?" by Chuck Hawley in THE ALASKA JOURNAL 9 (3) (Summer 1979): 14-23

MAP ACTIVITY

Trace the Iditarod Trail from Seward to Nome on the map below. Mark on the map the following spots that the lesson mentions along the trail:

1) Seward   2) Girdwood   3) Knik   4) Susitna   5) Skwentna   6) Takotna
7) Iditarod   8) Dishkakat   9) Kaltag   10) Unalakleet   11) Nome

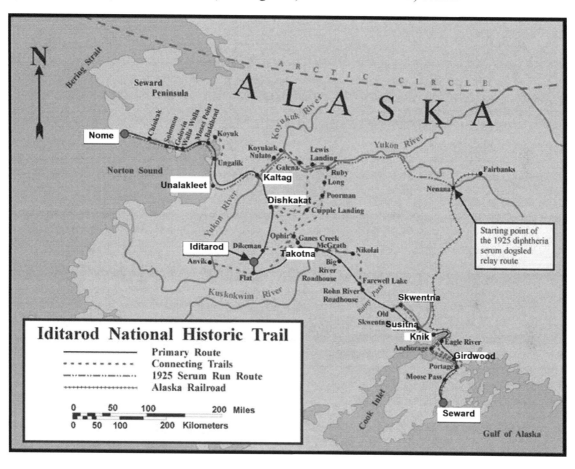

Places Along the Iditarod Trail
Word Search Puzzle Key
Find the words on the list below

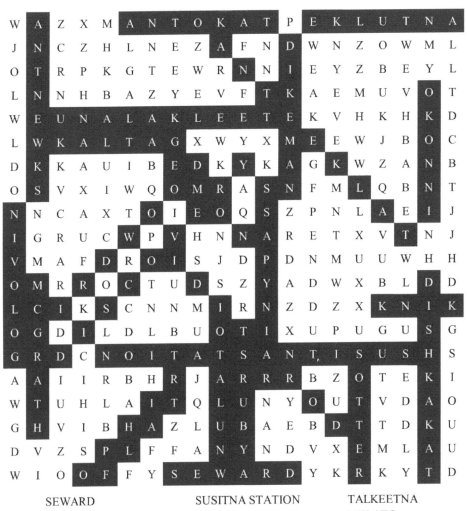

W	A	Z	X	M	A	N	T	O	K	A	T	P	E	K	L	U	T	N	A
J	N	C	Z	H	L	N	E	Z	A	F	N	D	W	N	Z	O	W	M	L
O	T	R	P	K	G	T	E	W	R	N	N	I	E	Y	Z	B	E	Y	L
L	N	N	H	B	A	Z	Y	E	V	F	T	K	A	E	M	U	V	O	T
W	E	U	N	A	L	A	K	L	E	E	T	E	K	V	H	K	H	K	D
L	W	K	A	L	T	A	G	X	W	Y	X	M	E	E	W	J	B	O	C
D	K	K	A	U	I	B	E	D	K	Y	K	A	G	K	W	Z	A	N	B
O	S	V	X	I	W	Q	O	M	R	A	S	N	F	M	L	Q	B	N	T
N	N	C	A	X	T	O	I	E	O	Q	S	Z	P	N	L	A	E	I	J
I	G	R	U	C	W	P	V	H	N	N	A	R	E	T	X	V	T	N	J
V	M	A	F	D	R	O	I	S	J	D	P	D	N	M	U	U	W	H	H
O	M	R	R	O	C	T	U	D	S	Z	Y	A	D	W	X	B	L	D	D
L	C	I	K	S	C	N	N	M	I	R	N	Z	D	Z	X	K	N	I	K
O	G	D	I	L	D	L	B	U	O	T	I	X	U	P	U	G	U	S	G
G	R	D	C	N	O	I	T	A	T	S	A	N	T	,	I	S	U	S	H	S
A	A	I	I	R	B	H	R	J	A	R	R	R	B	Z	O	T	E	K	I
W	T	U	H	L	A	I	T	Q	L	U	N	Y	O	U	T	V	D	A	O
G	H	V	I	B	H	A	Z	L	U	B	A	E	B	D	T	T	D	K	U
D	V	Z	S	P	L	F	F	A	N	Y	N	D	V	X	E	M	L	A	U
W	I	O	O	F	F	Y	S	E	W	A	R	D	Y	K	R	K	Y	T	D

SEWARD	SUSITNA STATION	TALKEETNA
INNOKO	KALTAG	NULATO
OPHIR	TAKOTNA	MCGRATH
NOME	GIRDWOOD	EKLUTNA
KNIK	SKWENTNA	RAINY PASS
DISHKAKAT	UNALAKLEET	GOLOVIN
IDITAROD	FLAT	DISCOVERY
OTTER	DIKEMAN	RUBY

UNIT 7: A FEW TRAILBLAZERS

LESSON 23: BEACONS IN THE WILDERNESS

FACTS TO KNOW

Tributary – A stream that flows into a larger stream or lake

Arthur Harper – One of three early pioneers who set up strategic supply posts along the Yukon

Jack McQuesten – One of three early pioneers who set up strategic supply posts along the Yukon

Alfred Mayo – One of three early pioneers who set up strategic supply posts along the Yukon River

COMPREHENSION QUESTIONS

1) What led Jack McQuesten to the Yukon?

McQuesten remembered that in 1871 he was wintering on the headwaters of Hay River with some companions, doing a little trapping and trading with the Indians. "We had heard a great deal about the Yukon River from men who were in the Hudson's Bay Company employ and we concluded we would go and see for ourselves what the country was like," he wrote. (Pages 247-248)

2) What early pioneers did McQuesten meet up with on his way to Fort Yukon?

Arthur Harper and Jack McQuesten ran into one another at the mouth of Nelson River. He arrived in the company of Al Mayo and George Nicholson at the fort on July 21, 1873, six days after the Harper party. (Page 248)

3) Why were Russian explorers, the Hudson Bay Company and Alaska Commercial Company uninterested in gold?

They were more interested in trading fur than seeking gold. (Pages 248-249)

4) What did the men learn when they attempted to obtain information about the tributaries of the Yukon River? How did Jack McQuesten and Arthur Harper make a living in the Yukon?

When they attempted to obtain information about the tributaries of the Yukon River, they found little knowledge had been gleaned since Russian occupation. By 1873, less than a dozen white men inhabited the length of the Yukon, and they were concerned with furs, not gold. McQuesten and Harper made a living by prospecting and fur trading. (Page 249)

5) What important contribution did Jack McQuesten, Arthur Harper and Al Mayo make to the Yukon gold rush?

The string of posts they set up along the Yukon, their grubstaking others and providing advice where to prospect, as well as the credit they extended, helped many prospectors. The men realized that their most important task was to establish a reliable source of supply. It was impossible, they had discovered, to carry on systematic prospecting without an assured source of provisions and miners' supplies. (Pages 252-258)

DISCUSSION QUESTION

(Discuss this question with your teacher or write your answer in essay form below. Use additional paper if necessary.)

Jack McQuesten, Arthur Harper and Al Mayo never became rich from their famous work in the Yukon. What do you think this trio gained by their work?

_____
_____
_____
_____
_____
_____
_____
_____
_____
_____
_____
_____
_____
_____
_____

ENRICHMENT ACTIVITY

Spend some time reading the Website for the Alaska Mining Hall of Fame at http://alaskamininghalloffame.org. See how many names you recognize from your study of Alaska mining history on the Inductees page.

LEARN MORE

Read more about Al Mayo by visiting http://alaskamininghalloffame.org/inductees/mayo.php

UNIT 7: A FEW TRAILBLAZERS

LESSON 24: VOICE OF THE YUKON

FACTS TO KNOW

Robert Service – A famous English poet who wrote about life in the North
Whitehorse – The capital city of the Yukon that inspired Robert Service to write his first poems

COMPREHENSION QUESTIONS

1) Famous humorist Will Rogers, who was proud to be a "_common_ man," said that Robert Service served the _common_ man "_literary steak_ well seasoned with plenty of calories and tasty trimmings!" Many of Service's poems were inspired by the _prospectors_ of the gold rush.

2) Where was Robert Service born? Where did he live most of his life? Why have Alaskans "adopted" him?
Although his life in the New World was spent mostly in Canada, the poet of the Yukon was adopted by Alaskans, too. For surely no one before or since has better interpreted the vastness, power, beauty and cruelty of the North. Service was born in Preston, Lancashire, England, of Scottish ancestry. (Page 258)

3) How did Robert Service end up in Canada? What did he do for a living before he began writing poetry?
At the age of 20, he quit his job in a bank, withdrew his savings and bought a steerage ticket to Halifax, Nova Scotia, to seek fortune in the New World. He kept traveling west, and by the time he reached Victoria, British Columbia, he had only a few dollars left. He worked for a while on a farm, and then he hit the road. He traveled up and down the Pacific Coast from Canada to Mexico working as a fruit picker, field hand, dishwasher — any job that came to hand. (Page 259)

4) What led Robert Service to begin writing poetry?
When he arrived in Whitehorse, he found a thrilling environment and began to write rhymes describing the North Country. Some people thought his rhymes had merit, and he was asked to write a poem to recite at a church function. He would take walks and the poems would come to him. (Pages 260-261)

5) What was the title of the first book published by Robert Service? What are some topics that Robert Service wrote about in his poetry?
He wrote about the beauty of nature that he saw while taking his walks. He wrote about the

tough life of miners. His first published book was "Songs of a Sourdough," printed in 1907, and later reprinted as "Spell of the Yukon and Other Poems." (Pages 261-264)

6) Name two of Robert Service's famous poems or books. How many poems did he say he wrote? What was his goal?
Some of his famous poems were: Call of the Wild, Rhymes of a Rolling Stone, Ballad of Blasphemous Bill and Good-bye Little Cabin. Two of his books were, The Spell of the Yukon and Other Poems and the Trail of '98. He once stated that he had written more than 800 poems and his goal was 1,000, "if the Lord of Scribes will spare me to finish the task." (Pages 262-270)

DISCUSSION QUESTION

(Discuss this question with your teacher or write your answer in essay form below. Use additional paper if necessary.)

Why were many Robert Service fans surprised when they met him? How was his demeanor different from his poetry?

_____
_____
_____
_____
_____
_____
_____
_____
_____
_____
_____
_____
_____
_____

ENRICHMENT ACTIVITY

Spend some time in nature with a notebook and pen like Robert Service. See if you can write your own poem about what you see, smell, hear or touch. Don't worry about making it perfect. Enjoy the creative process.

LEARN MORE

Read more about Robert Service and his poetry by visiting https://www.poetryfoundation.org/poems-and-poets/poets/detail/robert-w-service

UNIT 7: A FEW TRAILBLAZERS

LESSON 25: SOURDOUGH PREACHER PAINTER

FACTS TO KNOW

Eustace Paul Ziegler – Missionary to Cordova and famous artist
Sourdough – A nickname for someone that spends the entire winter north of the
Arctic Circle (also a name used for long-time Alaskans)

COMPREHENSION QUESTIONS

1) How old was Eustace Paul Ziegler when he arrived in Cordova? Why did he travel
there?
He was 22 years old when he traveled to Cordova to take over St. George Mission built by
Rev. E.P. Newton, an Episcopal minister based at Valdez. (Page 273)

2) Describe the Red Dragon. What kind of people did it attract?
The Red Dragon was a bright red building in the middle of many of saloons. Everyone was
welcome. Before its warm, friendly fireplace, wastrels and gentlemen, workers and strays
gathered to sleep, wrangle, fight, read, visit, sing and play the piano. (Page 274)

3) How did one painting for sale in a drug store change the direction of Eustace Paul
Ziegler's life?
He received a telegram saying that one of his paintings had been sold for $150 to E.T.
Stannard, president of the Alaska Steamship Company. Stannard later asked Ziegler to do
a series of murals for the company's Seattle offices. When the murals were completed, the
Zieglers returned to Cordova, but new offers flooded the little Alaskan minister. (Pages
276-277)

4) What kind of subjects did Eustace Paul Ziegler paint? Which famous mountain was
one of his favorite subjects to paint?
He was painting the natural beauty he saw in every direction, and the people around
him – the trappers, fishermen, prospectors and Natives of the Copper River Valley and
all over Alaska. One of his most famous paintings was the "Arctic Madonna." The
Eskimo mother and her placid baby won innumerable prizes and hung in many galler-
ies. For years, Ziegler traveled about Alaska seeing and painting everything he could.
One of Ziegler's favorite subjects was Denali, which he often called "his studio." (Pages
275-278)

DISCUSSION QUESTION

(Discuss this question with your teacher or write your answer in essay form below. Use additional paper if necessary.)

One of Eustace Paul Ziegler's famous quotes was, "If you don't paint for money, you'll make money." What do you think he meant by this statement?

_____

_____

_____

_____

_____

_____

_____

_____

_____

_____

_____

_____

_____

_____

_____

_____

LEARN MORE

Read more about Eustace Paul Ziegler and other artists who found their inspiration in Alaska by visiting http://www.akhistorycourse.org/americas-territory/alaskas-heritage/chapter-4-19-art-literature-science-cultural-institutions-and-recreation

TIME TO REVIEW

Review Chapters 20-25 of your book before moving on the Unit Review. See how many questions you can answer without looking at your book.

This photo of Eustace Paul Ziegler, 87, was taken shortly before his death in 1969.

Early Alaska Trailblazers
Crossword Puzzle

Read Across and Down clues and fill in blank boxes that match numbers on the clues

Across

2 Mayo's name is associated with this village

4 Russian governor who forbade anyone from leaking information about gold being found in Alaska

6 Ancestry of Robert Service

9 Eustace Paul Ziegler drew artistic scenes upon these

10 Distributing point for people exploring possibilities of fur and gold along the Yukon River

14 This was the first building in Cordova

20 Ed Schieffelin's sternwheeler that became a supply carrier for trading posts

22 Eustace Paul Ziegler's profession when he arrived in Cordova in the early 1900s

23 People who wander from place to place without a home or job

25 Traders and prospectors hunted this wild animal for its meat

26 A poem or song narrating a story in short verse

28 People who mine for gold and other precious metals

29 A person living in unsettled country

32 Settlement where McQuestern said he and his companions were treated like kings

33 Editor of the *Whitehorse Star* who encouraged Robert Service

34 One of three men who became traders in the Yukon Basin in the 1870s

35 He was known as the voice of the Yukon

36 The meager stores along the Yukon River in the 1870s belonged to this company

Down

1 He was the first to discover gold in the Yukon in the 1870s

3 People who buy and sell goods

5 When Robert Service was transferred from Whitehorse to this town he found himself a celebrity in the eyes of the townspeople

7 A person who makes a new track through wild country

8 Fort that McQuestern established in 1870s six miles down from where Dawson was born in the 1890s

11 A person who is among the first to explore or settle a new country or area

12 People Robert Service found when he arrived in Whitehorse in early 1900s

13 A newcomer or novice, especially a person unaccustomed to the hardships of pioneer life

15 One of three men who became traders in the Yukon Basin in the 1870s

16 Another term for Alaska

17 Nickname of Episcopal mission in Cordova

18 Man who convinced Ziegler to follow his passion for painting

Early Alaska Trailblazers
Crossword Puzzle Key

Down (Continued)

19 Eustace Paul Ziegler became famous for doing this activity
21 Famous poem written by Robert Service
24 An old-timer in Alaska is called this
27 Writing that is arranged with a metrical rhythm, typically having a rhyme
30 A group of lines forming the basic recurring metrical unit in a poem
31 Eustace Paul Ziegler was known as this to everyone who knew him

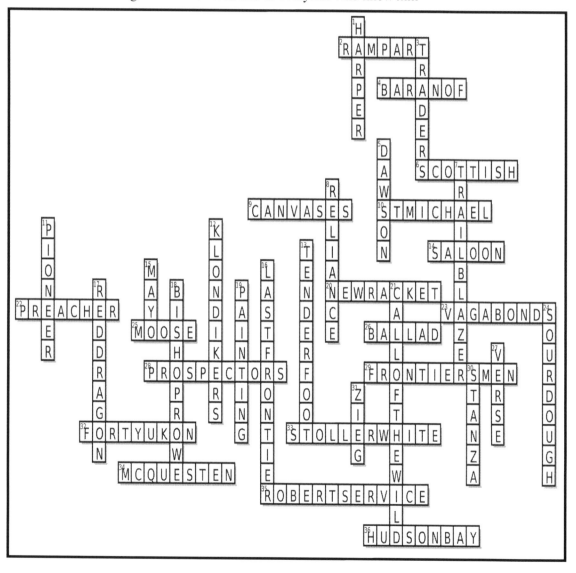

UNIT 6: WILDERNESS TRAILS
UNIT 7: A FEW TRAILBLAZERS

REVIEW LESSONS 20-25

Write down what you remember about:

Sled dog team – _A group of dogs trained to pull a sled for travel_

Lead dog – _The dog that leads the sled dog team_

Iditarod Trail – _The approximately 1,000-mile route from Seward to Nome_

Walter Goodwin – _Hired by Alaska Road Commission to scout a trail from Seward to Nome_

Tributary – _A stream that flows into a larger stream or lake_

Arthur Harper – _One of three early pioneers who set up strategic supply posts along the Yukon_

Jack McQuesten – _One of three early pioneers who set up strategic supply posts along the Yukon_

Alfred Mayo – _One of three early pioneers who set up strategic supply posts along the Yukon_

Robert Service – _A famous English poet who wrote about life in the North_

Whitehorse – _The capital city of the Yukon that inspired Robert Service to write his first poems_

Eustace Paul Ziegler – _Missionary to Cordova and famous artist_

Sourdough – _A nickname for someone that spends the entire winter north of the Arctic Circle (also a name used for long-time Alaskans)_

Fill in the blanks:

1) _Natives_ of Alaska, northern _Canada_, Greenland and Siberia used dogs as _winter draft animals_ for centuries. _Russians_ arriving in western Alaska during the 1700-1800s found _Alaska Natives_ using dogs to haul sleds loaded with fish, game, wood and other items.

2) Early _Russian_ fur traders added _handlebars_ to sleds and trained _lead_ dogs in order to use dog teams as a means of transportation through Alaska's wilderness.

3) When gold was discovered along the _Innoko_ River around 1906-1907, another trail was forged that would become one of the most famous _sled dog_ trails in history – the _Iditarod_ Trail.

4) Maj. Wilds P. Richardson ordered _Walter Goodwin_ to blaze a route from _Seward_ through the Cook Inlet country and beyond to _Nome_. From January to April 1908, _Goodwin_ and a three-man crew scouted and blazed a trail from _Seward_ to Susitna and then west through Rainy Pass, across the Kuskokwim Valley to the _Innoko_ Mining District, which included Ophir, McGrath and Takotna. They then angled the trail _northwest_ across the marshy lowlands of the Innoko Valley and connected with the _Yukon_ trail at Kaltag.

5) The town of _Iditarod_ grew out of the wilderness after prospectors _John Beaton_ and _William Dikeman_ discovered gold along the Haiditarod River, a _tributary_ of the Innoko, in December 1908.

6) Three early pioneers, _Arthur Harper, Leroy Napolen "Jack" McQuesten_ and _Alfred Mayo_ traveled into Alaska's interior and found a lack of _supply centers_. Had they not seen the need to establish _supply centers_ in the wilderness, it is possible that _gold rushes_ to the Yukon and Alaska would not have boomed.

7) When they attempted to obtain information about the _tributaries_ of the Yukon River, they found little knowledge had been gleaned since _Russian_ occupation. By 1873, less than a dozen white men inhabited the length of the Yukon, and they were concerned with _furs_, not gold.

8) As _Robert Service_ looked out the windows of the train heading to _Whitehorse_ from _Skagway,_ he viewed the rugged trail that led to the Klondike gold fields. The sensitive young man found it a thrilling environment and began to write _rhymes/poems_ describing the _North_ Country. He was asked to write a _poem_ to recite at a _church_ function.

9) He wrote something every day on his lonely _walks_ along the trails. He looked foward to those _walks_, he said, because he knew the _voice would whisper in his ear_, and he would bubble verse like an artesian well, composing "The _Spell_ of the Yukon" and many other ballads.

10) _Eustace Paul Ziegler_ was only 22 years of age when he arrived in Cordova to take charge of its Episcopal mission nicknamed the _Red Dragon_. He decorated the walls of the _Red Dragon_, and the church that was later built, with _paintings_ of great beauty and deep religious feeling.

11) The president of the _Alaska Steamship Company_ asked Ziegler to _paint some murals_ for the company's Seattle office. When the _murals_ were completed, the Zieglers returned to _Cordova_, but new offers flooded the little Alaskan minister. He finally had to make a choice between the _ministry_ and a career as an _artist_.

12) One of his most famous _paintings_ was the "_Arctic Madonna_." The _Eskimo_ mother and her placid _baby_ won innumerable prizes and hung in many galleries. His sympathy and affection for the _Native_ people of Alaska shines through his _paintings_.

Traders like Jack McQuesten, pictured here in the early 1900s, made it possible for prospectors to get supplies and that allowed them to continue their search for gold.

UNIT 6: WILDERNESS TRAILS
UNIT 7: A FEW TRAILBLAZERS

UNIT TEST

Choose *three* of the following questions to answer in paragraph form. Use as much detail as possible to completely answer the question.

1) Why were sled dog teams an important means of travel in early Alaska? Name some of the ways that they were utilized.

2) What important trail was Walter Goodwin hired to scout in Alaska? Why is this trail one of the most famous trails in Alaska history? Where did it start and end?

3) What need did Jack McQuesten, Al Mayo and Arthur Harper fill in the Yukon? Why was this vital to the success of the gold rush?

4) How did Robert Service begin his poetry career? How did he go about writing his poetry? Name two of his famous poems.

5) Describe Eustace Paul Ziegler's journey from missionary to Cordova to painter. What kind of paintings was he famous for?

_____

_____

_____

_____

_____

_____

_____

_____

_____

_____

_____

_____

_____

_____

_____

_____

TEACHER NOTES ABOUT THIS UNIT

UNIT 8: MIGHTY MOUNTAINS

LESSON 26: ELIAS – TOUGH EVERY FOOT OF THE WAY

FACTS TO KNOW

Mount St. Elias – The second-highest mountain in North America – it is located on the border of the Yukon and Alaska

Summit – The peak of a mountain

Israel Cook Russell – The first to explore Alaska for the U.S. Geological Survey

The Duke of Abruzzi – The first to summit Mount St. Elias

COMPREHENSION QUESTIONS

1) Who was the first non-Native to spot Mount St. Elias? When did he first see it and name it for Russia?
Vitus Bering discovered and named it for Russia in 1741. (Page 281)

2) What important areas are located around Mount St. Elias?
The area around Mount St. Elias contains an important grouping of Athabascan prehistoric and historic archeological sites of the Tlingit and Eyak Indians and the Chugach Eskimos, including Taral, Cross Creek and Batzulnetas. (Page 282)

3) How tall is Mount St. Elias? Why is it considered one of the greatest snow climbs in the world? *According to the Coast Survey Triangulation in 1892, it is 18,024 feet tall. Capped with snow and draped with glaciers that wind upward and back as far as the eye can see, the mountain, according to many mountaineers, presents the greatest snow climb in the world. (Page 282)*

4) Although Israel Cook Russell never reached the peak of Mount St. Elias, what important discoveries and accomplishments did he make on his two trips?
His team found and named new peaks and glaciers. They studied the movements of the glaciers and made a general topographical reconnaissance of an unknown region. (Page 284)

5) Who was the first to summit Mount St. Elias? When? How long was the expedition?
In 1897, Italian Duke of Abruzzi was the first to summit Mount St. Elias. The expedition occupied a 50-day roundtrip from the coast, mostly spent in bad weather, carrying or hauling loads in deep snow, across and up the glaciers. The duke's expedition was carefully planned, and he showed himself a capable leader, as well as an experienced mountaineer. (Pages 285-286)

6) Why did Asa C. Baldwin lead a party to climb Mount St. Elias? What was different about his approach to the mountain?

Asa C. Baldwin led a party to climb Mount St. Elias when the International Boundary between Alaska and Canada became a question of importance after the discovery of gold in the Yukon. Unlike the other expeditions that went in from the Pacific side, the Baldwin party attacked inland, going in from McCarthy in the Copper River valley. (Pages 286-288)

DISCUSSION QUESTION

(Discuss this question with your teacher or write your answer in essay form below. Use additional paper if necessary.)

Climbing large mountains like Mount St. Elias is a dangerous endeavor. What were some of the challenges that the climbers faced?

ENRICHMENT ACTIVITY

Imagine that you are a mountaineer who is preparing to summit a mountain. Considering what you have learned from this lesson, what do you need to do to prepare? What type of supplies do you need to bring with you? Write a short paragraph about how you will prepare for your upcoming climb.

LEARN MORE

Look for this article at your local library:
"Wrangell-Saint Elias: International Mountain Wilderness," Alaska Geographic Society, Vol. 8, No. 1, 1981.

UNIT 8: MIGHTY MOUNTAINS

LESSON 27: DENALI – THE HIGH ONE

FACTS TO KNOW

Denali – Also known as "Mount McKinley," this is the highest mountain in North America

Dr. Frederick A. Cook – Controversial mountaineer who claimed to have summited Denali and discovered the North Pole

Admiral Robert E. Peary – U.S. Navy engineer who claimed to be the discoverer of the North Pole

Walter Harper – An Athabascan Indian, he was the first person known to have climbed to the summit of Denali

COMPREHENSION QUESTIONS

1) Who named Mount McKinley? Why did he choose this name? Why is the name controversial? _William A. Dickey, a prospector, named the 20,320-foot mountain for presidential nominee William McKinley of Ohio in 1896, even though McKinley had no ties to Alaska. Controversy surrounded that name from the get-go and continues today._ (Page 293)

2) Who was the first white man to climb Mount McKinely? How did he and his companions raise money for the trip? _Judge James Wickersham and four companions made it to about the 10,000-foot level in 1903. The men had raised money for the adventure by issuing a newspaper and selling advertising. Lacking equipment but swamped with business, Wickersham, who was 45 at the time of the attempt, wrote that the fellows churned out an eight-page Fairbanks Miner "on the first printing press ever brought to the valley – a typewriter."_ (Page 294)

3) In 1903, _Dr. Frederick A. Cook_ and five team members reached the 11,300-foot level of _Denali_. He and a team returned in 1906 to climb it again. Cook later reported that he had summited _Denali_ that time. After returning from Alaska, _Cook_ gave lectures about his achievement – including one in Seattle that started the organization of _The Mountaineers_. He left his 1903 and 1906 book manuscripts with a publisher in 1907 and then headed for Greenland, a trip that later evolved into an expedition to reach the _North Pole._

4) Why did some people doubt Dr. Frederick A. Cook's account of his expedition?
His vague description of his ascent route and a questionable summit photo of his guide shown standing on top of an outcropping of rock that was somewhat pointed in appearance, led many to doubt his claim. The guide whom he alleged went to the top of Mount McKinley with him announced that they never had been to the summit and that the picture Cook took with Barrill holding a flag on the top was miles from the peak. (Pages 296-298)

5) What led the Sourdough Party to decide to climb Denali?
A group of men called the Sourdough Party, which included Tom Lloyd, Charles McGonagall, Pete Anderson and Billy Taylor, set out to conquer the mountain in 1910 because of a barroom bet between Tom Lloyd and bar owner Bill McPhee. (Page 302)

6) Who was the first person to summit Denali? Who led his team, and why did this man refuse to call the mountain Mount McKinley?
Athabascan Walter Harper, son of pioneer Arthur Harper, was the first person to summit Denali. Rev. Hudson Stuck, Episcopal archdeacon of the Yukon, led the team. He refused to call the mountain McKinley out of respect for the Native people who named it Denali many years before. (Pages 304-308)

DISCUSSION QUESTION

(Discuss this question with your teacher or write your answer in essay form below. Use additional paper if necessary.)

In 2015, the U.S. Geological Survey announced that new measurements put Denali's height at 20,310 feet, 10 feet shorter than previously measured. That same year, President Barack Obama officially changed the name of the mountain to Denali. Do you think it matters whether we call the mountain Denali or Mount McKinley? Explain your answer.

ENRICHMENT ACTIVITY

Learn more about Denali National Park by watching this 5-minute video on YouTube: https://www.youtube.com/watch?v=TiJtxItuC18

LEARN MORE

Look for this book at your local library:
The Ascent of Denali, Hudson Stuck. Seattle: The Mountaineer, 1977.

UNIT 8: MIGHTY MOUNTAINS

LESSON 28: KATMAI ERUPTS

FACTS TO KNOW

Novarupta – Volcano in Southwest Alaska that erupted in 1912 and was largest volcanic eruption of the 20th Century

Mount Katmai – One of five vents encircling the Novarupta volcano that has a central lake-filled caldera formed during the Novarupta explosion

Dora – Little mail boat that brought the first news of the eruption to the outside world

Kodiak – The closest sizeable town that was only 120 miles away from the eruption

Valley of 10,000 Smokes – The valley within Katmai National Park and Preserve that is filled with ash flow from the eruption of Novarupta June 6–8, 1912

COMPREHENSION QUESTIONS

1) Who were the only eyewitnesses to the volcanic eruption in 1912? How many people lost their lives during the eruption?
The Natives of Savonoski and Katmai were the only eyewitnesses. Most authorities say no lives were lost in the 1912 eruption, although Merle Colby claims about 200 Natives in remote villages in the path of the ash fall died. (Page 311)

2) Describe what some of the eyewitnesses saw and heard during the Novarupta blast.
American Pete, Savonoski's village chief, said, "The Katmai Mountain blew up with lots of fire, and fire came down trail from Katmai, with lots of smoke." D.F. Howard said, "...Early in the afternoon, I heard a series of heavy explosions ... increased until it resembled the continuous roar of a heavy canon barrage." Many eyewitnesses reported rocks and small stones falling from the sky. (Pages 310-312)

3) Where was the *Dora* sailing when its crew spotted the eruption? Describe the crew's account.
On June 6, the Dora was sailing into Kupreanof Strait between Kodiak and Afognak islands when crewmembers noticed a huge, dense cloud rise over Mount Katmai. It spread northwestward over the sky and masses of volcanic ash settled over the sea. It became so dense the captain had to bypass Kodiak. "... lurid flashes of lightning glared continually around the ship ... birds floundered, crying wildly through space and fell helpless to the deck." (Pages 313-314)

4) What horrible experience did the people of Kodiak endure when Novarupta erupted?
Terror and fear held the island's 400 inhabitants in a grip of smothering ashes and volcanic fumes for days. None of the people who went through those days fail to mention the awful darkness, which was described as something so far beyond the darkness of the blackest night that it cannot be comprehended by those who did not experience it. (Page 315)

5) U.S. Revenue Cutter *Manning* carried more than 500 residents of *Kodiak* and *Woody Island* to safe waters during *the massive eruption in June 1912*. The priest of the Greek Orthodox Church told his people that if the *church bells began to ring* they were to go down to the dock.

6) Who was the man that made the Valley of 10,000 Smokes known to the world? What are two things that we learned from him?
Robert F. Griggs. Griggs' summary of events stated there were first premonitory symptoms, especially earthquakes, sufficient to warn the Natives. More than 40 times the amount of material dug in the greatest excavation ever attempted by man — the Panama Canal — was thrown into the air. All the buildings of all the boroughs of greater New York City wouldn't fill Katmai's crater. (Pages 319-321)

DISCUSSION QUESTION

(Discuss this question with your teacher or write your answer in essay form below. Use additional paper if necessary.)

Imagine that you lived in Kodiak at the time of the eruption at Katmai. Remembering the accounts that you read in your lesson, how do you think you would have felt during and after the eruption? Can you imagine experiencing constant darkness like they did?

_____

_____

_____

_____

LEARN MORE

Explore the Valley of 10,000 Smokes by visiting https://www.nps.gov/katm/planyour-visit/exploring-the-valley-of-ten-thousand-smokes.htm

TIME TO REVIEW

Review Chapters 26-28 of your book before moving on the Unit Review. See how many questions you can answer without looking at your book.

UNIT 8: MIGHTY MOUNTAINS

REVIEW LESSONS 26-29

Write down what you remember about:

Mount St. Elias – *The second-highest mountain in North America – it is located on the border of the Yukon and Alaska*

Summit – *The peak of a mountain*

Israel Cook Russell – *The first to explore Alaska for the U.S. Geological Survey*

The Duke of Abruzzi – *The first to summit Mount St. Elias*

Denali – *Also known as "Mount McKinley," this is the highest mountain in North America*

Dr. Frederick A. Cook – *Controversial mountaineer who claimed to have summited Denali and discovered the North Pole*

Admiral Robert E. Peary – *U.S. Navy engineer who claimed to be the discoverer of the North Pole*

Walter Harper – *An Athabascan Indian, he was the first person known to have climbed to the summit of Denali*

Novarupta – *Volcano in Southwest Alaska that erupted in 1912 and was largest volcanic eruption of the 20th Century*

Mount Katmi – *One of five vents encircling the Novarupta volcano that has a central lake-filled caldera formed during the Novarupta explosion*

Dora – *Little mail boat that brought the first news of the eruption to the outside world*

Kodiak – *The closest sizeable town that was only 120 miles away from the eruption*

Valley of 10,000 Smokes – *The valley within Katmai National Park and Preserve that is filled with ash flow from the eruption of Novarupta June 6–8, 1912*

Fill in the blanks:

1) _Mount St. Elias_, the first point sighted by white men on the mainland of Alaska in 1741, has proved a mighty challenge to _mountaineers_. Only a handful of climbers have conquered it in the years since the Dane, _Vitus Bering_, discovered and named it for _Russia._

2) In 1890, professor _Israel Cook Russell_ led a party composed of Mark B. Karr and six camp hands. Russell and Karr undoubtedly would have reached the top if a _severe storm_ had not forced their retreat.

3) But the route that professor _Israel Cook Russell_ had explored was of great assistance when, in 1897, the mountain finally was conquered by one of the world's most distinguished mountain climbers and explorers, _the Italian Duke of Abruzzi._

4) Rising more than 20,000 feet above sea level, a mountain known to early _Athabascan_ Indians of the Interior as _Denali_, meaning "_The High One_," towers over all other peaks in its mountain range.

5) _William A. Dickey_, a prospector, named the 20,310-foot mountain – which is said to have one of the earth's steepest vertical rises – for presidential nominee _William McKinley_ of Ohio in 1896, even though he had no ties to _Alaska_.

6) At a dinner sponsored by the National Geographic Society, with a seething _Admiral Robert E. Peary_ in attendance, President Theodore Roosevelt hailed _Cook_ as the conqueror of McKinley and the first American to explore both _polar regions._ But critics soon denounced _Cook's_ claim and suggested his summit photo of Ed Barrill was suspect.

7) The Natives of _Savanoski and Katmai_ were the only eyewitnesses to the most spectacular _volcanic eruption_ to occur in North America during the 20th century. Native residents of _Katmai_ village found their barabaras – Native dwellings – buried in _ash_ from the 1912 _eruption_ of _Novarupta/Katmai_.

8) The _Dora_, the intrepid little mail boat that had had a share in almost every adventure in _Southwest_ Alaska, brought the first news of the _eruption_ to the outside world. Crew members noticed a huge, dense _cloud_ rise over Mount _Katmai_. It spread northwestward over the sky and masses of _volcanic ash_ settled over the sea. It became so dense the captain had to bypass Kodiak.

9) A news dispatch from Cordova, 360 miles northeast of the _eruption_, reported that many people received _painful burns_ when a heavy rain mixed with the _ash_ in the air to form sulfuric acid.

10) The closest sizable town, _Kodiak_, was 120 miles away from Mount _Katmai_. Terror and fear held the island's 400 inhabitants. None of the people who went through those days fail to mention the awful _darkness_, which was described as something so far beyond the _darkness of the blackest night_ that it cannot be comprehended by those who did not experience it.

The members of the 1919 National Geographic Expedition that explored the Katmai region following the eruption of 1912 found volcanic rocks, called pumice, so light that they could balance them on their legs.

Mighty Alaska Mountains
Word Scramble Key

Unscramble the words below

1.	ituvs nigbre	vitus bering	This Danish explorer discovered and named Mount St. Elias for Russia in 1741
2.	stcaahbana	athabascan	Prehistoric and historic archeological sites of these Indians were discovered around Mount St. Elias
3.	gsarciel	glaciers	Rivers of ice
4.	onintreemau	mountaineer	One who climbs mountains
5.	wne royk simte	new york times	This company funded the first attempt to climb Mount St. Elias in 1886
6.	ocrfcanes	francesco	This duke was the first man to summit Mount St. Elias in 1897
7.	naffamuk	kauffman	First woman to summit Mount St. Elias in 1946
8.	eht ghhi one	the high one	The meaning of the Athabascan Indian word Denali
9.	aalaks	alaska	Denali is part of this mountain range
10.	rocaevvun	vancouver	This English explorer made the first known reference to Denali in 1794

Mighty Alaska Mountains
Word Scramble Key – Continued
Unscramble the words below

11. dykeic	dickey	Prospector who gave the name Mount McKinley to what we call Denali in 1896
12. whkmiearcs	wickersham	First white man to attempt to climb Denali in 1903
13. ocko	cook	Controversy surrounds this mountaineer's claim that he reached the summit of Denali in 1906
14. gudsrhuoo patry	sourdough party	This group of men attempted to climb Denali in 1910 based on a wager
15. uodsnh ukstc	hudson stuck	Episcopal archdeacon whose party was the first to reach the summit of Denali in 1913
16. rarphe	harper	Name of Athabascan Indian who had the honor of being the first to step foot on the summit of Denali first
17. smtayaclc	cataclysm	A large-scale and violent event in the natural world
18. onarvpaut	novarupta	Name of volcano that exploded in southwest Alaska in June 1912
19. odkaki	kodiak	Name of town that was covered in ash for days following the eruption in Katmai
20. nngmnia	manning	Name of ship that saved the people of Kodiak and Woody Island from the deadly ash that fell in June 1912 following the eruption of a volcano

UNIT 8: MIGHTY MOUNTAINS

UNIT TEST

Choose *two* of the following questions to answer in paragraph form. Use as much detail as possible to completely answer the question.

1) Why was Mount St. Elias such a challenge for even experienced mountain climbers to summit? What were some of the challenges that the mountaineers had to face? Describe one expedition that you read about in Lesson 26. Was it successful?

2) Explain why the name "Mount McKinley" is controversial. What other controversy did you read about in Lesson 27?

3) What happened in Kodiak in the summer of 1912? Describe some of the eyewitness accounts you read in Lesson 28.

TEACHER NOTES ABOUT THIS UNIT

TEACHER NOTES